G000117856

# THE RISING
# COST
## OF STAYING ALIVE

MARTI LAURET

BY THE SAME AUTHOR

Be Careful What You Wish For
And other Stories

For Josh

Splash go the genes

into the pool and

up you come, spluttering.

Wonderful.

# TABLE OF CONTENTS

## THEN

## LATER

# IF NOT NOW, WHEN?

# THEN

# HELLBENDER

Dozing in a deck chair in spring sunshine is just about the best thing ever. Sunday afternoon in shorts and a halter top with the warm sun just kissing your shoulders and your thighs and your middle. Drifting into a dream, sensing the call of blue jays and the endless buzz and chirp of cicadas, Meg let herself slide into perfect peace. If she never knew bliss again, she felt it in the brief moments before a warm dream enveloped her.

Howling before she was awake, she doubled over. Something sticky struggled and writhed against her bare tummy and down her shorts and thrashed against her knees. The deck chair held her briefly prisoner until she threw herself open-eyed into the grass, pushing with palms that squirmed to get away from what they touched until she was freed of it, lying on her side, shrieking to the sound of Boney laughing. He was shrieking too, and already running away in case she jumped onto her legs and came after him. Boney was 10, just, and Meg was 9 – but she was bigger than him and if she got him he was in for it.

Boney needn't have worried much. She was too horrified by what she saw squirming in the dandelions to uncurl herself. It was something so ancient and yet so forceful that she lay on her side daring to watch. She tried to force the flailing thing to assume a shape she could make sense of, but it writhed so wildly she couldn't fix it with her eyes.

She thought for a moment that it looked at her with its thick end, out of a tiny black dot the size of a single buckshot. This peppercorn eye was separated so far from its mate that it seemed to look at her side on, and all the while its whole long length flashed and flipped and flailed among the smashed grass blades. Meggie caught sight of what looked like a tiny hand for a moment and then it flipped round and the thin end snapped like a whip. A five-toed foot showed itself for a second but only for a second.

'Boney, you little snotty shit! What the hell is that?' Boney was dancing up and down at the end of the yard, laughing and shrieking and pointing at her and at the thing he had offered to her bare body in its skinny shorts.

'Gotchoothattime, gotchoo, gotchoo,' he was all ten year-old mania and beyond explaining.

Meg got to her feet and stared down at the creature. It was brick-brown, about two feet long, with what she guessed was a flat head at the thick end and weird frills along its oozy sides. Sure enough, it had tiny four-toed baby hands near that end, and down by the tail, long skinny-toed five-fingered slanty feet at the back. Its tail mashed the weeds back and forth and left a wake behind.

'It's a hellbender,' he gargled through his laughter. She brushed at her shorts and stared. Boney amplified, 'devil-dog.'

A shape appeared at the kitchen door of the house, and Meggie's mother stepped down into the yard. 'I heard some words I didn't ought to hear. You children are big enough to know that you only say 'hell' and 'devil' if you're reading out loud from the Bible,' she pronounced. Then, '*What the hell is that?* Charlie! Come out here and tell me what these children have brought into my yard.'

There was a delay.

Eventually Meggie's father shambled over the step and peered down into the weeds. 'Well my good Lord, where did you get that hellbender?'

Boney sidled up behind Meg, giggling 'It's a snot-otter.' To Meggie's dad he said, 'Underneath of them flat stones in the stream in the woods. I brought him home in a tackle box.'

'Well you are going to pick him right up and put him in the box and take him back where you got him. He could die out here in the sun. If I was your daddy I'd take a switch to you, now go on. *Go on – git.*' Boney grumbled up with the fish-box that contained a slosh of stream water and wrestled the hellbender into it, left them, mumbling sassy words all the way to the gate that let on to the woods.

Monday morning Boney and Meg shared a seat on the yellow school bus. Meg saw a fumbling movement in Boney's book satchel, but he knew she wouldn't tell. 'Is it still alive?' she whispered.

'Course,' Boney was complacent. 'I put a cup of water in the satchel and some night-crawlers from Daddy's bait-box for him to eat. Wait'll recess comes. I'm gonna scare them girls with him.'

He never made it as far as recess. Delania Jackson told Mrs. Oliver that there was a funny smell coming out of Beauregard's book satchel and Meggie got caught passing a note to him that his dish was cooked.

'Mary Grace Biggler and Beauregard Bradley! Y'all are in this together.' Mrs. Oliver snatched up the bag and drew the occupant out by its limp tail, a few night crawlers clinging to its sides. 'You killed this creature and you're going to take it home and bury it. But before you do, both of you are going to stay in all recess and write this 200 times.' She wrote some dreadful long words on the board and the chalk broke just she got to the end.

Cryptobranchus Allegeniensis

Mrs. Oliver had not trained as a biology teacher for nothing, even though she was stuck here at East Gant Elementary School.

'Ma'am?'

'Yes, what?'

'Does it have to be joined up writing?' Boney wasn't good at cursive.

'Yes it does. And you may as well know that what you have brought into my classroom is or was a living fossil dating back 160 million years from what you may call the Jurassic Period. If your parents let you learn the evolutionary explanation,' she hastily added. Not everybody is allowed to learn stuff like that.

'I'm gonna be a long time forgiving you for this,' Meggie hissed. She wrote the Latin words carefully at first, making sure to get the spelling right. Then she scrawled them a bit so that the words drifted up above the lines on the paper and then fell below them like a skip-rope flopping up and down. Boney took no notice of her. He screwed up his eyes and concentrated on the shapes of the letters.

She said, 'Boney, I'm gonna kill you.'

He was not alarmed. Boney was thinking that his letters on the page looked silly and it was hard to get the shapes right. Also that covering his tracks was going to be a problem. He'd have to carry the satchel in through Meg's front gate and out by the back of their yard so as not to be seen by his mother. If she saw him taking the book satchel into the woods she'd know he wasn't going down there to do his homework. He'd have to sneak out of Meggie's and put the creature back in the stream under a pile of rocks. If Meggie's dad said anything he'd have to go on pretending that he had taken it, still alive and thrashing, back to the stream yesterday like he was told to.

Underneath all those concerns, another fleeting thought reached his consciousness, retreated, and hovered just beneath the surface. He tried to concentrate on the letters dancing in front of him on the blackboard, and painfully worked at recreating their shapes on his paper.

'I said, I'm gonna kill you.'

'Meggie, don't.'

'Don't what? Don't kill you? Why shouldn't I, you little snot-rag?'

He couldn't explain. He drew in his elbows as tight as he could to his sides, still writing, making the letters smaller. He crossed his legs and then his ankles, curling his left hand around his poor writing so she couldn't see and laugh at him. She could tell he was feeling bad.

'All right, don't be a scaredy-cat,' she said. 'I'm not going to really kill you.'

Silence.

'And I'm not going to tell.'

'I don't care if you do,' he almost whispered.

Meg whisked away at the paper, easily penning perfect round vowels and sounding out the syllables in her head. She knew something was wrong with Boney but she didn't feel like worrying about him. It was more fun to imagine the words as a clapping game: Cryp-to-bran-chus—clap-clap-clap! Allegeniensis—clappy-clappy-clap-clap! Or... could you jump rope to it?

It could be even better than Mississippi which everybody was getting tired of now.

'*Mi-double s-i*

*double s-i*

*double p-i!*'

She muttered the skipping-rope liturgy under her breath as she wrote the last few lines at the bottom of the next page. 'Aren't you finished yet?' she asked him, just for the sake of meanness. She could see he was only halfway down the final page. Meggie went to the window and pushed it up. Mrs. Oliver could be seen through the ground floor window, doing playground duty. 'Ma'am!' Meggie called out, 'I'm finished! Can I come out now?'

'No you may not, Mary Grace. I said all recess and I meant just what I said.'

Meggie shut the window, just a little louder than was necessary. She danced about, pretending to skip rope. The trick was to skip on one foot leftwards over the descending rope and change over when it was on the up stroke and skip to the right as it came down. Skip, skip.

Boney ground his teeth and kept on scratching at the paper until the bitter end. He barely spoke to her, for longer than just the rest of today. He drifted away from her for a week, and then a week more, spending longer and longer on his own, down in the woods. He lay on his stomach in the oak leaves, lifting the layers and watching the bugs. White wormy ones crawled out of rotten wood, and if you watched them every afternoon for days, they turned into beetle things and others wrapped themselves up in gauze and went to sleep. He hunkered down by the side of the stream, watching the fish sliding and dancing in their silver silence along the eddies.

Eventually he got up his nerve and lifted up the pile of rocks he'd placed over the dead body of the hellbender at the beginning of the summer. Carefully he lifted out what was left of it, what had not been eaten. He dug a hole with his hands in the deep loamy earth and placed the head and bones in the hole, whispered briefly that he was sorry, and covered it up.

That fall, Beauregard's parents decided he'd better go to the Catholic school. Although long-lapsed, they could scramble up enough of a connection to get him in. The teaching was better there than it ever was at East Gant. Eventually he learned to read and write properly.

Meggie moved away. He heard his mother say that her mother had popped in to say goodbye before the movers came.

# THE JEWELLED DISH

There was a small jade dish on the end table by the sofa. That's where it always lived.

The dish was enameled underneath, and curved upwards at the edges. The upper surface was inlaid with pieces of coral and lapis encased in a thin layer of clear glass. In the centre of the dish a lit cigarette rested. Smoke rose in a straight line through the strutted frame of a linen lampshade and emerged above it, ascending to the ceiling.

Lucille sat on the carpet and watched quietly as the smoke rose.

Seated on the sofa, her father turned a page in his book. There was a fractional movement in the air and the thin smoky line wavered. Without lifting his eyes from the page, Lucille's father reached for the cigarette, picked it up, and drew on it. The smoke went in and down, down, and was absorbed, and exhaled. The cigarette was ground out on the glass surface.

Years from now, a thoracic surgeon would remove her father's vocal chords, encrusted as they were with pearlescent nodes. Lucille would wash and polish the dish, place it under the lamp, and see it glow in a new silence.

# UNDER THE ICE

All the popular girls wear Jantzen twin sets with white cotton collars at the neck. You have to wear them with a pencil skirt and saddle shoes with white socks. If you can't be a popular girl you can dress like one, only you have to work at an after school job that gives discounts to buy the stuff. Unless you have rich parents. Or unless they're in the military and you can shop at the PX on the Little Creek Naval Base. That's what Barbara Sharkey does.

Or: I can reduce my mother to a nervous wreck by nagging at her relentlessly to give me the money – until finally she goes out to work to buy me stuff. She tries so hard to please me it makes me feel a little bit sick.

Hattie is here, cleaning the glass panes in the big doors facing the dock. It'll be another hour or so until Mama and Dad get home from work in town. I watch Hattie, and as she peers at the smudges on the glass, I look beyond her at the dock, and the Lake. Mama pays Hattie to be around so I'm not alone when they're at work. Hattie does the jobs around the house that Mama has given up trying to make me do. On the shore I can see Donnie, our collie. He and Bingo, the collie-cross from next door, have found something wriggling in the water. A half-dead perch or a water snake.

Last summer I went seine-netting with John Grandy, the little 10 year-old kid who lives down our unpaved bumpy lane. He loves to throw his nets out into the Lake where they hang suspended from cork floats and then he slowly pulls them in. The Lake is full of wild stuff. When he catches minnows, the ones that are never going to grow big, he takes them home in a jar. But if he catches baby perch or bass he always puts them straight back in so they get to grow up. He's good like that.

John's too young to go to our school. But Mama said his parents are going to send him to private school next year anyway, because of the integration. Just in case coloured kids start coming to Princess Mary High School where I go. Seems a little bit stupid, when Hattie's here all day in our house. What's the difference if her kids go to our school?

I'm looking at the Lake but I'm not thinking about John Grandy and his pollywogs any more. I'm remembering how disappointed I was when I tried for the cheerleading squad and I didn't get picked. They have the try-outs in September every year and the two gym teachers, Mrs. Bartok and Mrs. Horton, line the hope-fuls up in groups of nine or ten and then Mrs. Bartok names a cheer you don't know which one she's going to name, and then she snaps her fingers and you all start doing the moves and saying the cheer. She'll say, 'Vic-tory!' and snap. All the girls try to start at just the right moment, and you do the hand moves and the foot moves and if it's that one you shout out,

*'Victory, Victory is our cry:*
*V-I-C-T-O-R-Y!*
*Are we in it? Well I guess!*
*Will we win it? Y-E-SSSS!!!'*

As you shout out the Y-e-s you have to arch your back and leap as high as you can with your arms above your head and then you hit the ground lightly on the balls of your feet and bounce. If you were doing it for real you'd have pom-poms in your hands. I should know. I practiced all summer and I still didn't make it because I'm not that popular.

Dad was nearly driven crazy by all that practicing. I used to do it all day when I was hanging around the house. One Sunday night I heard him muttering to Mama that he'd 'had about enough of all that *petit-bourgeois* teenagery' whatever that is. Neither of them understands at all how vital it is to be popular at Princess Mary. If you're not popular nobody speaks to you in the halls between classes, the boys don't date you, and nobody sits with you in the lunch-room. And the teachers know who's popular. They think it's just as important as we do because it makes for school spirit and good behaviour. It's a whole world and either you're in it or you're dead.

Maybe next year I'll make the cheering squad. And at least I got into Beta Alpha which is a decent enough sorority. It's about the second best at the school. That's not bad.

It's wintertime now. Christmas soon. It's Friday and tonight the Lake might freeze over. Hattie has gone home, Mama and Dad are back and Mama is cooking supper. I watch her, but she's given up on making me learn to cook. After supper Dad will race me to the sink because in one of his weak moments I got him to agree to pay me 50 cents if I'll wash dishes, but he doesn't want to part with the money. Then I go to bed in the little bedroom under the eaves. I can see stars over the Lake. They're the last things I see. Mama calls to me to turn off my radio but I just can't yet, because Jimmy Reed is singing 'Down in Mississippi' and that's a dirty-boogie black song that means something else.

I wake and look out the window. Sure enough, the Lake is frozen. I can see John Grandy standing at the end of our dock. He's holding two pairs of ice skates and calling me 'Carolyn!'. I throw on something woolly and hurtle down the stairs, knowing I can borrow his mom's ice-skates. The dogs are going crazy barking and sliding around on the ice. John and I are skating in big circles on the bumpy ice. Mama comes out and slides around with us and laughs as though she was a kid again. Jantzen sweaters and cheer-leading are all forgotten. This is the very best, best part of living in Virginia. Things freeze over. Who knows what's going on underneath?

# SOMEBODY'S SON

The man's neck was precisely as broad as his face, giving him the look of a raw sausage if you felt like looking at him. There was usually a half-smoked cigarette behind his right ear, as an insurance against want. A pair of thin gloves would be jammed into a back pocket in case an opportunity arose for taking something without leaving any signs behind. By about lunch time he would have shoe-horned his ass into a pair of urine-spotted jeans. They had the sort of knees about which people said, 'Those pants are the only holy things about him,' as he was never seen in a pew at the Assembly of God on a Sunday morning. There was a rolled-up Confederate flag in the cab of his truck, but he hadn't made it to the Klan rally in Louisville – not because he'd had a change of mind or heart, but because the truck wouldn't start. So he swore for a while and went on over to Montgomery's to spend the last of his gas money on a couple six-packs of Coors Light. That was yesterday, but it could've been any day, pretty much.

We found his body in a ditch in the red clay at the bottom of Kite Hill. Maybe he just fell over and knocked his head on a rock. He could have drowned easy in 6 inches of water.

# DARLENE'S HOUSE

◦

She is in Darlene's house for the first time. There is a smell of dog hair and human sweat, wet nappies forgotten and stuffed into maggoty cupboards. The biggest of the hound dogs is curled on an ancient rag rug at the feet of the biggest person, Darlene's Pa, shirtless. His wife, Mama, slumps in a corner of the couch. One end of it is propped up with bricks. Mama stares at nothing, as Pa rolls a cigarette from a loose tobacco can displaying the feathered headdress of a Cherokee chief.

Carolyn knows none of them can smell what she smells, because this is what it's like to live here. Darlene is unaware, and unembarrassed. Her 5 year-old sister lies on the rug, her arm around the dog's neck. Tomorrow he will lead the hunt in the Dismal Swamp. Tonight and always they all live in this low-ceilinged room. A door stands open, leading to a bedroom heaped with unwashed clothes. Beyond this, bit of a bunk bed frame, then darkness.

'Your daddy was shocked when he saw inside their house,' Carolyn's mother said later.

But Carolyn knows, you smell it before you see anything.

# BLOODY SNOW

W eetabix with hot milk... school lunch box ...cut the bread, spread the marg, then the Marmite 'Are you nearly ready, Bren?'

Where's my school socks? Mum, look out the window Anni looks out. God, he's right. Where's the footpath? Where are the shrubs? It looks as if snow drifts are up to the sills. The Today Programme witters in the background as she peers through a patina of ice on the window.

From the radio, 'In Derry yesterday about 4 p.m. more than two dozen civilians shot, 10 so far reported dead.' The milk boils over and she swipes the saucepan off the flame. There is a smell of burning milk and a pool of grey-brown residue forms around the gas burner. 'The shooting took place at Free Derry Corner. Parachute regiments were dispatched to make arrests and firing began —'.

There is a loud knocking and a jiggling of the door latch. Rupert Ward-Smith, son of their landlady, thrusts his head around the door. 'School's closed,' he announces, entering without invitation. The boys are gleeful. Radio news rattatats over their voices and Anni is suddenly aware that these shootings haven't happened in some remote corner of the world. It is Northern Ireland and British troops are killing civilians. 'Rupert, did you have breakfast already?'

The door is thrust open again and there is a freezing draft of air. Rupert's mother Isabelle is in the doorway. 'What luck!' she gestures outside. The shed door stands open and there are the parallel tracks of two sledges Isabelle has dragged behind her. 'We're going sledging on the Downs. Come on, boys, mittens and hats, get ready!' A pair of black labs is rioting in the drifts, challenging each other with front paws flattened, hind legs on springs, tails up.

Tennyson Downs on the Isle of Wight, threaded with footpaths through the heather, resembles a Siberian steppe. Hills slope upwards to the cliffs and beyond them a sea of blue glass. It is a perfect day. As Anni and Brendan bundle into their outer clothes, six year-old Rupert pushes past them just far enough to grasp a double handful, squeezes, and with perfect aim launches the first snowball of the morning. It splatters across Brendan's narrow chest, and for a moment Anni sees the bullet from an SLR rifle, someone falling, hears the sound of screaming with her inner ear.

Tearing through the gate and up the hill with the others, she releases the image into this perfect day. Let today be, she thinks. Just have it. Give it to Brendan.

Gasping and laughing together they reach the summit, shrieking at the boys not to go near the edge. The cliffs lie beyond, under the snow covering brush and grass. She feels her heart stab, sees the risk, and just in time the boys see it, taking their cue from the dogs. Animals know better.

The blades of the sledges are gleaming. Rupert and Bren plunge onto them and together Anni and Isabelle launch their boys down the hill and away from the silver cliffs. Far below them are the white-quilted roofs of Alum Bay House, annexe, garage, grounds, sheds all sparkling. Trees around them with branches drooping, laden. Boys shouting, dogs barking and leaping up through drifts, shaking snow in the boys' faces, plunging again into the snow. Again and again Anni and her landlady shout encouragement, cheer on their racing children. They are two women with their kids, no longer rich and poor, landlord and tenant, all differences merged.

And for a moment, just a moment, because it's 1972 and 'The Troubles' seem so close, Brendan's name, his Catholic grandparents and their Irish parents all entwine for a millisecond, she sees blood on the snow. While Irish mothers are howling in horror, can there be a perfect day? 'Yes!' she insists. There has to be. For Brendan's sake, this has to be a perfect day 'Come on all. Hot chocolate! Who wants one?' Joyful, breathless children head for the main house, Isabelle tall, striding down the hill in her big boots, followed by her dogs, then the boys, and finally Anni. She makes a silent promise: the radio will be turned off today. It will stay off.

# PARAPORTI

---

There's a ship in the back yard. I wake up in the little attic bedroom and I'm looking out the window at a huge naval vessel. As I lie there under the sheet it looks as if the Lake has been replaced by a ship and it's sitting at the end of the dock.

People say we're lucky to live here, with a small fresh water lake by the back door and the Chesapeake Bay only 200 yards down the road. You take it for granted, where you live. We can ice skate on the Lake in winter and hear the waves crashing on the beach at the same time.

Today is a day worth screaming about, and I do. I call out to Mama and Dad downstairs. If they're still asleep they won't have seen it. It doesn't take them long to scramble out of bed and race to the windy end of the dock in their bathrobes. They're Oh-my-godding and going 'Would you believe it' and the phone is ringing because John Grandy and his parents have seen it too by now.

Mama and Dad are hustling into their clothes and talking on the phone. Dad is talking to Walt Grandy about calling the Coastguard. I'm pulling on shorts and a work shirt that a man left here last summer. It says 'Price's TV Center' on the back. I knot it at the waist and grab the phone as soon as Dad hangs up. I call Carolyn. Carolyn Canning is my best friend. We tell each other all our secrets and never stop talking even when we're going to the bathroom. She has to know this. She has to come down here and run all the way.

We all go down to the beach in a gang, scrambling over the dunes and down to the hard sand. There is this gigantic ship stuck there on the beach. Dad and Walt Grandy are talking in their grown men's voices about north-east gales and vessels running aground but Mama and Anne Grandy and I are just staring upwards with our mouths open. John Grandy is only 8 and he doesn't want to be with the women and the men aren't talking to him.

On the side of the ship is its name: *Paraporti*. There are men in uniform, sailors and what looks like officers shouting down to us but I think it's a foreign language and the wind is hurling away their words.

Carolyn catches up to us, panting and staring and saying she can't believe her eyes. Because we're 14 and have no manners and no decorum we are jumping up and down and shouting to the sailors but they can't hear us and we can't hear them.

After a while we're too hoarse to shout anymore and Dad and Walt are saying they want some coffee and somehow we straggle off the beach. We can't leave it for long though, because we have to see what happens next. Dad finds out from the Coast Guard that the ship is an Argentine training vessel for midshipmen and there are plans to pull it off the shore.

Back on the beach the wind has dropped a bit. Dad has some Spanish and manages to make himself heard. The young midshipmen are crowded together at the bow of the ship, and they get us to understand that they are not allowed to '*desembarcar*'. But their *Capitan* says we can come aboard! Wow! Who would believe it?

They lower a kind of aluminium ladder down the side. The kids are trying to clamber onto the ladder but Dad and the Grandys are grown up enough to realise that the tide's coming in and even if the water's not deep enough to lift the Paraporti off the sand, it'll be too deep for us to climb off without getting soaked. Somehow he makes this clear to the Argentinians and they haul the ladder back up again, making gestures like sad shrugs and much good will and all that.

Back at home we eat baloney sandwiches and work out when the time of the next low tide. Anne Grandy has gone to their house to make a batch of brownies for the sailors. Mama likes Anne and sits on the beach with her a lot. They talk pleasantly about whatever women talk about when their kids aren't around. *Their stuff.*

Right now I'm not thinking about anything but getting onto the ship.

Down at the beach the tide is out and oh joy there's no sign of the Coast Guard. The Paraporti is still right where it was. Some of the men in uniform come to the side and call down to us. Dad gets it across to them that he has to go to work, but the kids can come aboard if accompanied by a parent. Mama says she's not going up that ladder, but Anne Grandy is game. She has the brownies in a back pack and scrambles up, John behind her going up just like a monkey. Carolyn is next, and me last. I don't like heights and it's very scary but I have to get up there, I just have to, have to, have to.

You're never going to believe this but it's true. The midshipmen have a record player in the mess and they are eating the brownies and playing Elvis Presley's 'You Ain't Nothin' but a Hound Dog'. They politely ask Carolyn and me to show them the dance called the jitterbug which we of course do. Gorge and Juan were our favourite dishy midshipmen. They were most respectful and applauded us when we did our dance.

The Coast Guard tugs came at high tide the next day and we waved them off. Carolyn Canning cried. She wanted to marry Juan. The wind blew him to us and the Coast Guard stole him away.

Years later, Margaret Thatcher ordered the sinking of the General Belgrano. I was sick at the thought that Gorge and Juan might have been officers on board as it went down.

# CADILLACS AND SHOTGUNS

I'm gonna study law and someday go into politics. That's my aim. Being a mechanic is just one step on the way. I don't drink and I'm putting the money away. One day nobody will know I sleep on a mattress in the attic with my two brothers. They won't ever hear that we had to lay a plank across the joists to get to the hatch and down the ladder into the house. That's where my four sisters are sleeping on cots and sofas, the baby's in a bureau drawer. We live on greens and grits, mostly. But it won't always be this way.

Where I work the sales guys try to keep us out of the showroom. They call us grease monkeys, I've heard them saying it. They think we're stupid and that we can't hear through the wall between showroom and the garage where we service the cars.

But we can hear most of it. There's a customer, a little funny looking fellow with a crewcut and googly eyes who comes most days to see if the Caddy Fleetwood his Daddy ordered is in yet. 'When's it coming'?' he keeps sayin'.

He never shows up with a friend, and he drives what must be his Mama's car, a little Chevy coup, a woman's car. I go up to him smiling and offer to park his car, make conversation because of the Cadillac. His Daddy came here twice, once to order the car and once to sign the form. Debbie in the front office had a copy of the order all ready and I made up a wage slip question so as to have an excuse to go in there and have a look. He'd signed the paper as Douglas F. McManus. On the order paper was my dream car. A 1958 Fleetwood 60 Special 310 horsepower.

After that I keep my eye out for the little fellow whenever he turns up. It's easy because he always comes on his own and he loves talking about cars. It never seems to bother him that I have axel grease under my nails and my overalls are never clean. When he looks at me he sees a friend who's a car guy. One day I tell him my name's Billy Vann and he says to call him Mac.

When the Fleetwood finally arrives it's even better than my wet dreams. It's black with polished chrome all the way down the sides and fish tails like the dorsal fins on sharks, each one topped with chrome. There was just one gold detail. On the hood above the fog lights, centered in between two pairs of headlights, there's a wide gold V with a royal crown medallion in the middle. You need sunglasses to look at it in the light. The car stands outside on the forecourt and I pretend to knock dust off it while checking out the interior.

When his Daddy is in the shop with the salesmen, playing the bigshot and writing the cheque, Mac waits outside. By now I'm his buddy and he's waiting for me. I say I'm pleased for him, but he says they're only going to let him drive his Mama's shitty little Chevy because this car is so... well, he doesn't even need to finish the sentence.

When they drive away, I think to myself, 'That's it.' They've got my dream car and I won't be seeing them or it ever again. I cross the road to the Seven-Eleven and get me a Dr. Pepper and a bag of potato chips just to have a reason to get out of the garage. I'm pissed off and it lasts all the rest of the day.

Weeks go by and I've almost forgotten the Fleetwood and the little guy. So I am kind of surprised when at closing time on a Friday, he drives up in it. My dream car. He grins at me like some cat with a goldfish and says to hop in. I leave my beat up old motorcycle in the garage and do just that. Can't believe I'm actually inside. It still smells new and the upholstery is button-down leather. This car even has air conditioning, god almighty and a German radio with a tape deck and Elvis is singing "Suspicious Minds".

Mac tells me that his Dad is on a business trip to Miami and Mac has got into the desk where the keys locked up. His Mama's off somewhere and we're princes of the road tonight. We pick up a couple of girls outside a bar on at the upper end of King Street and park by the side of the river. Neither of us got very far, but Mac's one gave him a phone number because he was driving the Caddy and he gives her a can of Bud.

We spend the last of that summer cruising around through a lot of beery sunsets. Mac tells me one night after a few that his real name is Thomas Frederick McManus Junior which is why he likes to be called Mac. Wouldn't anybody? He's been given the kind of name a big business man would have, the kind who sends his kid off to boarding school. But Mac has been a problem – he still is. He's just too little, and toothy, bog-eyed, weak. Sickly a lot of the time.

The pick-up girl turns out to be Linda, and she's as poor as me and mine. But Mac doesn't mind. After awhile she doesn't care about the car and she's really sweet on Mac. To him she's beautiful just because she's a girl and to her, well he's *nice* to her. He even gets all the way with her one night when we're down among the dunes, with the Fleetwood parked with two wheels on the road so it won't sink down in the sand.

Sometimes Mac falls into black moods and won't see anybody. Linda and I talk to each other outside the garage, because neither of us has a phone and we can't reach Mac.

One day she gets so desperate she goes around to his house, and everybody seems to be out. She has tears all down her face when she tells me she's found a door unlocked and she just goes on in to see inside.

There on the kitchen floor is Mac's body with a smooth bore shotgun lying by the side of him. She says there's blood and brains all over the window and on three of the walls. She finds the cartridge lying there too, and picks it up to remember him by.

It's in the local paper of course. 'Teen shotgun suicide. Parents devastated. Asking people to pray for them'.

I don't ever see the Fleetwood again. Linda and I got married three months later. She says she's glad she'll be eighteen, just, when the baby's born, which I guess is Mac's.

All this has set me back a lot, but one day I'm gonna study law and then go into politics. Linda's still got that cartridge, but now she's right behind me.

# LATER

# CONFLUENCE

'Hot tea in a *glass*? Well, well. I never heard of that before.'

'Here. I put the glass in a holder, with a handle. Like this. And sugar lumps in a saucer. Drink a little, then suck on the sugar. Like this, see?' Rochelle was pleased to use her samovar to make tea for a visitor. It happened so rarely. Her tiny apartment on the Lower East Side had room for few mementos, and she had few visitors.

Ruth tried to sip the steaming liquid, holding the silver handle between thumb and finger. The movement was unfamiliar. Like the taste – bitter, then so sweet. Her large, muscular hands, so sure when turning a patient in their bed at Bellevue, fumbled with the filigreed handle of the glass. 'But you know what? It's so nice to *be* here with you.'

'Yes. Yes, yes. After so many years at the Party Office, doing our work. Getting our papers out and addressing all those envelopes. We talk about Party business but we don't dare ask each other too many questions. I am old now. I don't care. I want to ask you... I don't know what.... Your job? What you do at that hospital?'

'Well that's easy. I do everything the doctors and the nurses don't do. And there's a lot to do, I can tell you. You know what Bellevue is of course. It's the New York City hospital for the mentally ill. Those poor folks who go crazy without any health insurance. Maybe some of 'em because they got no health insurance. Got nothing much of anything.

'I tend to the sick ones, the ones that can't get out of bed without somebody to help 'em, because I got a strong back. And I serve the tables, set the tables. Clear the tables. Wash about a thousand dishes. The other day one of the nurses said to me, "Ruth, that isn't the way," Ruth imitated a mid-western white woman's accent, "... that is just not the right way to set a table".' Ruth chuckled at the memory. 'I said to her, "No, I know the right way. It's the right way compliments of the U.S. Army".' Ruth grinned. 'That shut her up.'

'You were in the Army?'

'Yeah, there was a lot of black women in the War. They promised us training as nurses and medical technicians. But that's plenty about me. You tell me about you. Where you from? You Russian?'

Rochelle sighed. 'Yes, long ago. I was a child. My Russian things, the embroidery, the lace, they were in my Grandmama's box. My parents told me we were from a wealthy family, I can't remember. But my Papa had ideas from the liberals. Then he joined the Mensheviki. There was a civil war in the 20's. We had to get out. Many died, so many.'

'Your name... Rochelle Meadow?'

'I changed it, my mother said Meadow was good English word. Our name was Melekov. I was Raissa. My grandmamma called me that, Raissa. So long ago. Ach! America, so much money, and yet people are so poor. My father joined the Party here, and my brother too. They died. And we were all in jail. Now my son is married to a nice girl. She knows nothing. If I go to their house on Long Island he makes me put my Daily Worker in a sack.'

Ruth smiled. Drank the bitter tea. She was not about to remind Rochelle that the Worker hadn't been a daily paper in more than 20 years.

'You want a cheese Danish?' Rochelle hobbled to the cupboard and brought out the pastries, wrapped them each in a frayed Damask napkin.

'Let's cut one in half,' Ruth suggested, eyeing them for signs of age.

'But tell me a little bit,' Rochelle chewed, met Ruth's eyes briefly. 'Before the Army, where did you come from?' She meant, why do you look so strange, like an Indian with red skin and freckles on your nose and a Negro's hair?

Ruth, unoffended by her comrade's curiosity, grinned in answer. 'I'll tell you where I was from, and what made me join the CPUSA, but I'll keep it short. Don't wanna wear you out. You know New Orleans? Ever been there? Well it's got these big levees to keep out the Mississippi on one side and the Gulf on the other. My ancestors built those levees. They were African slaves working for the French. A lot of 'em met up with the swamp Indians and it looks like I'm descended from the results.' She laughed.

'My mama used to clean house for the white people in the city. Our name was Aguillard, but it was her name. I never knew my daddy. Mama spoke mainly Creole French. She used to call me Zwazo and my little brother was Bezwin. I was bird and he was bear.

'When the War came a lot of black women saw a chance. I didn't wanna do house cleaning and my brother was *never* cut out to be a butler, so we both joined up.' She took a deep breath, 'He didn't survive the War. But I was supposed to be trained as an army

medic. It would've changed my life. Well, it did that....
in a way. They call it 'This Man's Army' for a reason.

'There was no way they were going to let black
women do anything but orderlies' jobs,' she said.
'Cleaning up shit. We were so mad. At Fort Devens
where they sent us, there was a strike. Imagine that.
Black women on strike against the U.S. Army. Fifty-
seven of us refused to do any work at all when they
broke their promise to let us train as medics.

'In the end, they beat most of us down. But four of
'em Mary, Anna, Johnnie Murphy and Alice – they
stuck it out right to the end. They were court-martialed
and sentenced to a dishonourable discharge and a year
in prison with hard labour. After that I figured women
needed to be in the labour movement, after I left the
Army I joined the Party. So here I am. Sorry for the
long story.' A piece of pastry lay forgotten on the napkin.

'Stay longer, tell me more,' Rochelle urged her,
glad of the company.

'No thanks,' I gotta get on that subway and change
trains twice, get myself home and grease this crazy hair
down and get to sleep. Gotta get up at 5 o'clock in the
mornin' to get myself to Bellevue.'

Rochelle reached out a hand. Their fingers touched.

# ONION SKINS

Safely locked in the bathroom, Chahna touched the 'Reply' button on her phone. 'Yes, she typed, 'but 3:30, not 2:00. Have to do something with my family.' She hesitated, then touched the 'x' button and pressed 'send'.

Chahna was wearing a red V-necked tee shirt. On an impulse, she rose, and stood in front of the pink shower curtain. She touched her long hair, making sure it hung straight and even, framing her face, and re-moved a gilt necklace from a hook on the door. At the centre of the necklace was a charm in the shape of a dancing girl in a sari. This she laid on her forehead, drawing the necklace backwards towards the crown of her head. Then she took a selfie. She paused, and again she pressed 'send'.

This was Chahna's first act of planned disobedience. To carry out her plan she had to lie to her mother on a matter of importance, which meant lying indirectly to her father as well. Her parents were close, and they shared some remnant of the values they had brought with them from Karnataka in the north of India. She had agreed to see Jon, the Polish boy living next door. She was to meet with him on Saturday. Earlier today she learned Ammaji had arranged for the whole family to spend that very same Saturday afternoon in Muswell Hill, celebrating the 10th birthday of the daughter of a Dr. Sembhi, her father's friend and colleague.

Her mother had mentioned, too casually, that there were older children there. A boy was spoken of.

At only 18, Chahna knew she would be allowed, even required, to study law before marriage. 'But still, it never hurts to get to know new people,' Ammaji had said brightly. Chahna also knew that the frequency of these social engagements would increase as she reached marriageable age. She was also aware that her deepest wishes would lead her towards the performing arts and away from the arid world of tax law....

'Chahna!' Ammaji called up the stairs, 'What is the delay? Your father is home. We will be having dinner!'

The silent phone vibrated in Chahna's hand. She opened the text and there he was, pictured in high definition. Jon with his tan and curly golden hair. In her imagination he was gold all over. With regret, she pressed 'Delete' and raced down the stairs. It would be two whole days until she saw him again.

Chahna filled the days with college, staying as late as she could and returning to the family each evening. At home in the mornings the girls rose soon after their mother. Ammaji had to bathe before sunrise as she knew she could not worship or eat until she had done so.

On Friday morning, Chahna woke before her sisters and made for the bathroom ahead of them. Everyone hurried to work or to school in the mornings, and they agreed that a quick shower before *puja* was enough. Chahna needed more time in the bathroom than her sisters, but she did not dawdle. They knew Ammaji could not bear to rush the *puja* and for the sake of peace, they complied.

Chahna ushered her younger sisters before her: first 9 year-old Madhula, then Haimi who had turned 16, and now Chahna herself. They passed through the red silken curtains suspended over the doorway of a small upstairs bedroom. The curtains bordered above and below were worked with golden embroidery.

Facing them on the wall of the shrine was a gilt-framed picture of the triple goddess Lakshmi, Parvati and Saraswati. Parvati stood in the centre on the open petals of a pink lily. She wore a red sari and a gold crown bordered in emeralds. On her forehead, suspended from the crown, was the divine image of her husband Shiva, dancing. In her right hand, Parvati held a sword, and in her left, a bow and arrow. On her right side, her sister

Lakshmi, consort of Vishnu stood, holding a spear in one hand and a conch in the other. On Parvati's left side, stood Saraswati, goddess of knowledge and music, holding a small pink lily in her right hand and in her left, a musical instrument resembling a lyre. Other goddesses, with other arms, faded away behind them and beyond, into a glistening mist.

Silently, Ammaji waited for her daughters. When they were all there, she began *puja* by ringing a silver bell to let the god, God of all the pantheon of gods and goddesses, know of their arrival. Then she lit a candle on a lily-shaped stand and moved it silently in circles to light the shrine. She lit one stick of incense from the pot, and raised the cup of water offering the liquid in a wide-handled silver spoon towards the image of the triple goddess.

When she felt the blessing, Ammaji mixed a paste of *kum-kum* with purified water and gently touched her own forehead and the foreheads of each of her daughters. She smiled broadly at her girls. She took the *Prashad* from its silver dish surrounded by Shasta daisy flowers. God's food was strawberries today. Mother and daughters took the *Prashad* and they ate.

Madhula burst through the curtains and hurried back to her room, 'Has anybody seen my Magic Markers? My new ones? Mum, do you know where they are?' Haimi loitered behind her, as it's not cool to rush. On her way out of the front gate, she would wipe the goddess's mark of blessing from her forehead. Chahna lingered with her mother, wanting to hug her, feeling guilty in her anticipation of tomorrow. Guilty, and just a little nervous.

Saturday arrived. They had done *puja* and had a light breakfast, then homework, housework, and weeding in the herb garden. Ammaji was on her knees with a trowel and a sharp knife, cutting the tap root of a dandelion when the doorbell rang penetratingly from the front of the house. 'Chahna, Haimi! Can you answer the door?' Ammaji called to them. Haimi dawdled. Guiltily willing to oblige their mother, Chahna opened it.

Standing there on the front step, with a small boy and holding a younger girl by the hand, stood an English woman with a face vaguely familiar to Chahna. Behind them a boy of about 8 kicked at the row of seashells that Ammaji had used to line the sides of the front path.

Is your mum in?' the woman enquired. She was wearing a strappy emerald green top, white cut-offs, and flip-flops. Chahna could just see, at the edge of the woman's neckline, the inky tip of a rose. Bud, stem and presumably leaf, lost in flesh below the bra line. 'I'm Carole from number 18,' she observed. 'Had to bring the kids – Bob's down at the football club.'

'I wanna go to the football club,' said the boy. He kicked at the shells again.

'Stop that!' Carole admonished. 'He might take you to the match later if you behave. Stop that, Jason I said. I'll count to three one, two, three'. Jason withdrew the foot, but looked at it speculatively as if it might kick something unbidden. 'Sorry,' Carole turned back towards the open door.

'Hello, may I help you?' Hesitantly friendly, Ammaji stood beside Chahna, brushing the earth from her trousers.

'Yeah, only, I heard you teach Indian dancing?'

'Oh yes, yes! Come in. You are interested in Indian dancing? Yes, I can tell you anything you wish to know. Your children can play with my children. Chahna take the children with you, they can meet Madhula.'

Wordlessly, Chahna led the way upstairs to the girls' bedrooms. From the top of the stairs, Madhula sized the children up. The words, 'A girl too young to be of interest to me and a rather nasty-looking boy,' were written in her eyes for a second. Madhula vanished into the bathroom. Chahna sighed and led Jason and Maisie into the room she shared with her sister Haimi.

'Like, come in, why don't you?' Haimi rolled her eyes. 'Just what I always wanted when I've got an open bottle of nail adhesive in front of me.'

'There's nothing I can do about it,' Chahna lifted her shoulders. 'Ammaji is talking to their mother about Indian dancing.'

'Yeah. She's only too pleased to talk to anybody who'll listen,' Haimi spoke into the glue bottle. With resolution, she closed it and said, 'Well, do you guys like playing Mahjong?'

'What?' Maisie spoke from the glazed centre of her being.

'Never mind, come here. I'll show you some dolls I've still got from when I was little.' Chahna joined them and Haimi opened a box at the bottom of her wardrobe. 'This one is called Devi and this one is Geeta'

Voices floated up the stairwell. 'Indian classical dance is called Natyashstra, very theatrical. You show emotion through gesture, posture, and expressions of the face like so and hands like so. This we call *mudra*.'

'You what?' a voice answered.

'OMG! Haimi hissed, 'It's not that woman from across the road with the tattooed boob is it?'

'Hush,' Madhula intervened, 'hush, Haimi. Maisie, if this was your doll what would you call her?' Maisie held the doll tentatively.

Twang, twang! Suddenly there was a jangle of springs. 'Here, *you*!' Haimi's voice slashed at Jason, 'That's my *bed*. It's not a trampoline!' Enraptured, un-stoppable, he leapt repeatedly into the air. As they stared at him, Maisie slipped through the door, tried the locked bathroom, and proceeded down the hall to the next doorway.

Haimi grasped Jason and hauled him down the stairs in time to hear Carole say, 'Actually, I was looking for a belly dance class'.

'Belly dance?' Ammaji said vaguely. 'We don't do belly dance. There are many types of classical dance. I dance the Kathak which is from the North of India. But there are also others from Andra Pradesh, Manipur, Kerala, and many others'

'Oh well, thanks anyway. Here's Trouble,' Carole addressed her son, let's get your sister. Where did my daughter disappear to? Almost time for lunch – Maisie! *Maisie*, get here! Say thank you, and 'bye, bye.

'*Sukriya*,' Ammaji murmured, reclaiming her trowel. 'Chahna, will you see Mrs. Carole and her family to the door? Thank you, *sukriya*.'

They tottered down the path. With relief, Chahna followed. As they left, she knelt to straighten the white shells along the path, noticing the display of tiny yellow flowers whose roots were cooled by the shade of the shells. She was lost in thoughts of this afternoon, of later this afternoon, of Jon.

'I say, excuse me! This is Number One, is it not?'

What now? Chahna looked up. Proceeding towards her through the open gate was a heap of blankets with a graying head perched on top.

As it passed her and headed up the front step, the heap revealed itself to contain what must be a female form. It smelt of old, old cloth and dust and cat urine. Oblivious of the June sunshine, the heap's occupant made no attempt to get rid of the layers. A grubby hand was produced. Its nails were long and uneven, the nail beds and cavities filled with the detritus of years. In the hand was a kind of hat, knitted on needles of varying sizes, in wool drawn from the unpicked jumpers of past decades. The colours were a dirty mixture, like the swirled contents of a glass on a child's painting table.

'This *is* Number One. Good. Will you give this to Mr. Pook, please.' It was a polite instruction. Attached to the hat was a string with a begrimed paper label inscribed, 'Mr. D. Pook' in copperplate writing.

Uncertainly, Chahna took it. 'Who is Mr. Pook?' she asked. As her eyes traversed the pile of blankets, she saw that they overlaid a gentleman's threadbare overcoat. From a pocket of this coat, a mewling sound could be heard.

'You know Mr. Pook,' the woman said comfortably, 'the Duke of Edinburgh. He is Number One and he lets me call him Mr. Dukey Pook. You take his hat to him at the marina. You will find him on the Yacht Britannia.' An indulgent smile flickered.

From the pocket in the coat, the head of a small cat emerged, mewing. It had a long, scrawny neck and ragged sideburns of uncertain colour. The donor of the hat stroked the kitten and it began purring insistently, turning and twisting itself into the depths of the pocket.

'Thank you, my good woman. You will be rewarded by and by.'

From an upstairs window, Haimi peered. She aimed a look of contempt and mirth at the heap's retreating back. The mountain of wool strode away up the path, the gate swung closed, and it was gone. Chahna placed the hat in the recycling bin by the side of the house, brushing off her fingers and wiping them on her thighs. It was time to change her clothes, definitely time!

She washed herself again from head to foot and dressed conservatively, in Western style. She drew a soft leather bag from her wardrobe and placed in its depths a pair of jeweled thong sandals and a satin pouch containing a kohl eye pencil and some silver pearl shadow.

Stepping into a muted blue floral from Monsoon, she drew on shiny silken leggings that finished just above the ankle, and put leather pumps on her feet. Chahna knew that just now Ammaji would be devoting her attention to Haimi ('No young lady with false nails goes out of this house, you know that of course.') Downstairs, Madhula swung her legs from a kitchen stool. She had been ready for ages.

Apaji drove them all to Muswell Hill in their two year-old Nissan. He had had it steam-cleaned and polished for their visit to Dr. Sembhi's family.

At that house it was all the usual *Ahyeh*, welcome, welcome. Come in – Oh! Is that for us, and these! Oh, you are too kind, and hello there, come in, what's your name? Madhula, and what a pretty name! What lovely daughters, and *Ahyeh*, *ahyeh*, welcome, Dr. Naryan and Mrs. Naryan, and is this your eldest daughter? Ah, Chahna, and your sister is...? Haimi, Haimi well, come in and welcome.'

Of course it was Thank you, *sukriya, sukriya* and thank you very much, so good of you to have us, Dr. Sembhi and Mrs. Sembhi and all your children, hello, hello, Yes we found our way quite easily, we have been living in London so long, my husband knows it like the back of his hand of course. Such a lovely home you have, and who is this, and what is your name? How good of you, such nice manners. And are you the birthday girl? My, my, you are so tall for your age – such lovely children, all of them, Mrs. Sembhi—Yes, thank you, tea is perfect for me, such pretty china'

Chahna accepted tea. She sat and tried not to stare at anyone, at anything, to be modest and sit beside her mother. It suited her to let the mothers talk above her. There was another daughter of about 15 who welcomed Haimi into her room. Madhula stared about her with curiosity, asked impolite questions about all the ornaments and where they had come from. 'Staffordshire dogs! Well, think of that. And have you been to Staffordshire?' Ammaji placed a restraining hand gently upon her younger daughter who seemed intent upon turning the piece of pottery upside down to see it were hollow. 'Madhula! Where are your manners ?'

Head down, Chahna considered her next move. The two fathers began to speak of GP practice and the remarkable state of affairs with government funding and increasing patient numbers. They headed off towards some sanctum where ice tinkled. Trying his luck, the son followed. Eventually Mrs. Sembhi offered a tour of her kitchen, recently installed. With modest pride she spoke of '...these granite worktops, they can make your knives go blunt, you know'

An hour had dragged by. Time pressed. It was now or never. She drew her mother towards her as Mrs. Sembhi intoned about flagstone floors. 'Ammaji, it's started,' she whispered.

'What has started, my dear?'

Chahna fairly hid her face behind her hair, 'You *know* what!'

'A visit to the temple?' her mother enquired using their most private shorthand. 'You are not due until next week.'

'I can *feel* it, Ammaji. I have to go home. I have to go now.'

'Let's see if we can ask Haimi if she has anything'

'You know she doesn't. She isn't due until the week after.'

'These tiles came from a little shop we found in Kensington, and the paint is Farrow & Ball. I didn't care for the first colours, so we had to have it all done again'

'Yes, yes, Mrs. Semhi. I see. Most beautiful colours, most beautiful!' Softly, to her daughter she said, 'What are we to do? I can't ask your father to take you. It would humiliate him—'

'No, no. I'll get the bus home, Ammaji. There is a bus stop at the top of the road. It's only two stops. Thank Mrs. Sembhi for me, tell her I have a headache,' Chahna whispered frantically. Seeing her daughter in real distress, Ammaji gave way. 'Go then, I will take care of it all. Turn your jacket inside out and sit on it when you get on the bus.'

Chahna fled in shame. She had lost herself so completely in the lie that she felt she would bleed upon the pavement. Her heart raced, her breathing was shallow, but Jon was waiting, and she was off!

She reached the stop as the bus was pulling away and leapt on. Climbing the stairs she found a seat at the back. She made sure that the other passengers faced the front.

Then she drew the thong sandals from her leather bag. She exchanged her pumps for these, and took out a silky cosmetic pouch. Using a compact mirror, she applied creamy pearl beneath her brows and deepened the shadow under the bones with charcoal. Sure of hand, she lined each brown eye with kohl and glossed her lower lip. Seconds before the bus lurched, braking for the first stop, she was finished. Passengers got on, the bus heaved, and a gaggle of children pounded up the stairs. Chahna ignored them, gazed through the upper windows into suburban gardens.

The bus passed the second stop, and at the fifth she hurried down the stairs, darting from the open door. Steadying herself, trying not to think of the lies she had told her mother, she approached a park bench. The far end of the park was not far from the street where she lived with her family.

Apaji and Ammaji and her younger sisters were safely away, along with the Sembhis and their possibly *eligible* son. She had escaped for a couple of precious hours.

As she approached the bench, Chahna could see the back of a fair head and shoulders. He was there waiting. She slid onto the bench beside Jon, her dark hair curtaining her profile.

'Here you are,' he offered.

They spoke hesitantly at first, uncertain of their next moves. The very fact of meeting like this, a Hindu girl and a Polish Catholic youth, was both an achievement and a risk for each, even here in north London. In her family life, Chahna had known the simple irritants of sisterly argument and maternal prodding. She knew something of frustration, ruefulness, and affection with their father. But she knew nothing of wrath. She sensed an unknown danger.

Jon told her he lived with his lone father, and they grieved for his mother, two years dead of cancer. He had left school to work with his father as a general builder, sending money home to grandparents in Poland.

Chahna was impressed. She knew family life and was quick to sense devotion in another. They did not need to speak of the risk each faced, of disturbing the equilibrium in each family.

She wanted to share with Jon her passion for the performing arts. Her wish to express her talent was known in her family. But the expectation was for her to train in the law, indulging her artistic side only when she could. An accomplished wife who could earn good money and cook Punjabi style was a thing of value. She was loved. She was a commodity.

Jon surprised her by saying that, before they left Poland, he had been determined to be an artist. This came as a pleasing shock. She had believed him to be a handsome rustic with whom she might share her thirst for

self-expression. She wanted him to partake of her wonder. And found he had wonders and wishes of his own.

'What did you paint?' she asked him.

He laughed. 'At first it was faces on wood. Sheets of
MDF, plywood. I mixed shades of gloss paint and drew
and painted everything I saw, on anything I could get.
Then it was white emulsion mixed with food colours
and even vegetables to make the colours. My family
were always asking me, 'Jon, when will you stop that
and come and work?' To help my father, I would work
a few hours, but even then I would ... imagine? Imagine
what might be painted on walls and even saw faces on
round stones and wanted to paint them. From a child I
did this.'

'Do you still?'

'When I can. I have some canvasses now, and paper.
I am teaching myself water colour painting by watching
teachers on YouTube. I paint you several times.'

'Me? You painted me? From the selfie I sent you?'

'Thank you for the photo, but no, I drew you with
your family. You were walking away up the road, and
I painted all your long clothes, all different colours and
gold, shining.'

'We were going to a festival, wearing saris. You saw
us?'

'Yes, from the garden. I sketched and painted you
going away. With long black hair, swinging.'

She and Jon were walking north across the common. They had not touched. She was leading the way to the arts centre called Arcola. Here she gloried in minor roles in plays by amateurs, and saw, fleetingly, actors whose names were known all over London. She loved the buzz, erecting sets and taking them down, learning lines (not many, not yet) and dancing, embellishing the classical steps she had learned from Ammaji.

They entered the building. She could see Jon looking around him in curiosity. People spoke to her. Chahna smiled and lowered her eyes. She opened a door, and one of the smaller theatre spaces was before them. At the back of the stage, there was a painting which filled the wall.

At first glance, the painting appeared to be a giant copy of Leonardo da Vinci's Mona Lisa. There was the smile for which she is known, but she was wearing eye liner. The mystery of the smile, its wisdom and the calm gaze of the eyes behind which lay all the secrets of the world, were enhanced and distorted. On the forehead, above a red mark of blessing, was a pendant suspended from a gilded crown edged with green stones. The veil of a red sari fell away from the face. In her hand the painted woman held a pink lily. The area behind the Mona Lisa contained waterfalls as had its original, but the water fell in pools from which white buffaloes drank. Clouds floated in the background, and on these the word 'Ananku' appeared in English letters informed by shapes imported from the Punjab.

Chahna could see that Jon had never realised art could be like this. Or had he? She saw him studying the painted set, storing images to ponder.

She drew him away, pressed for time. It was essential to return home before her family got there.

They left and walked briskly across the common in near silence.

At the far edge, Jon turned to her. 'Please stop. I want to ask you so many things. Abruptly he sat on the ground, his sunny skin and hair framed by the dark, waxy leaves of laurel bushes at the park's edge. Chahna was enlivened by the pleasure of his company in her space. She had seen his wonder at the arts centre which was her cherished place. He had seen the set of the play she was rehearsing with other, older, Asian women. She said simply, 'I am glad you came with me.' She removed her phone from a pocket to take a picture. 'Stay still, just like that. I will have to delete it later. But for now, I want to see you just like this.'

Jon threw back his head and smiled full on at the camera in her raised hand. She saw his eyes were brown. Golden hair and brown eyes: *how beautiful.* His arms extended from short tee shirt sleeves. They showed the muscles of hard work, not the bulging biceps favoured by trainers at gyms, but the toughened forearms of someone who hammers and tightens and lifts and strains. She did not understand what she was looking at, but the sight delighted her. She took the picture, camera looking down on a healthy youth, seated on the grass.

'How do you dance?' he asked.

'Like this!' Chahna put the phone back in her pocket and arched her back, arms above her head, elbows bent. Each jeweled little finger touched its opposing thumb. She flexed her right knee, lowering her straightened body, then bent her other knee higher, resting its foot softly against the back of the flexed right knee. She smiled enigmatically and he saw again the expression of the Mona Lisa realised in the face of the goddess Parvati, wife of Shiva. Then she laughed and dropped to the ground beside him.

Filled with awe at something beautiful and unknowable, Jon did what young men of every country all over the world, and across every ocean and up to the snows of Himalaya and down to the tip of Terra del Fuego do, he leapt on her. Startled only for a second at the force and weight of him, Chahna lifted her face to his and they rolled over twice in the sunshine, knowing what they might do were it not for the open space around them where passers-by pretended not to see. She wriggled deliciously underneath him.

These feelings were not exactly new to Chahna, but much newer than Jon should know. With a stab of anxiety that cut through her rising blood pressure, releasing dread in her heart, Chahna saw beyond him the lengthening shadows of the trees. The family would be coming home. She had to go, *now*.

She wriggled up, Jon following regretfully after, and brushed the grass off her short skirt. A blade clung to the back of one of her silky leggings. They hurried away in the direction of their street.

Parting from the laurel branches, there appeared an ambulant heap of blankets. It was topped by a lank, grey mop of hair, and a mewing kitten could just be heard from somewhere beneath the layers of what might have been a rug or ragged coat. The figure reached down into the grass and retrieved a phone which lay there, partly covered by a bruised dock leaf. Its screen was dark. 'Mr. Dukey's girl,' the voice muttered, 'and away she goes with a pile of turkey feathers and a dandy candy sweet tooth cake, mmm.' The hand stroked the kitten and it purred, making room for the phone.

Chahna asked Jon to linger at the bottom of the road. She hurried home and threw open the front door.

Her family had reached the house before her. Sister Haimi stood in the hallway, with a lifted eyebrow.

'Chahna! Where have you been?' Ammaji's admonitory voice could be heard from the kitchen. 'I expected to find you lying on your bed with a hot bottle on your tummy and here you are coming in the door. If you were well enough to go walking about, you were well enough to have stayed at the Semhi house with us.

Something could have been devised! It was embarrassing for me.'

'Ammaji, I know. I just had to get some air after I got home. I got what was needed, *you* know, and then I took two paracetamol and felt better. I went to Arcola,' she leavened the lie with the yeast of truth and it rose and rose until she was mumbling about all the girls she had seen at Arcola and how they had delayed her and how they talked and how she had been waylaid on the common because someone let a large dog off the lead, then, full of holes, the lie flopped back down and she ran out of things to say.

'Well,' said Ammaji, remember not to take a shower until the third day after your visit to the temple has begun' Chahna cringed at the use of their shared euphemism for the blood of Durga. It was a betrayal to use their women's secrets as a cover for her own, more private, secret. 'and if you want to wash your hair, remember to do it in the bathroom sink. If Haimi and Madhula are in the bathroom you must wait and not—'

'We know, Mum,' Haimi intoned, 'drops from the wet hair of a bleeding woman must not touch the carrots being washed in the kitchen sink. If so, the carrots will be impure and the turnips will be impure—' this was delivered in a singsong voice, 'and fruit made impure must not be used for Prashad, nor any eaten at mealtimes dah-de-dah-de-dah....'

'Do not make light of our customs, bad girl,' Ammaji looked away darkly. Her expression showed regret for her bad girls, and regret that they had ever left Mysore.

A deep voice rang from the front room, 'She is home, we are home, it's good. Stop arguing in there.'

Ammaji laid her peeler on the draining board and joined her husband in the front room. She could barely be heard to say, 'You know Chahna is having her visit a week early this month. You are a doctor, should we worry?'

'I am not my children's GP or yours, you know. If you are worried, take her to the surgery.'

'I am worried now. I am most concerned about her. She is not herself.'

'If she is still at temple in two weeks' time she might be anaemic. Worry then.' He lowered his voice. 'Better she is at temple too early than not at all'

'Be quiet! I cannot believe you are saying such things. Just look what life in this country has done to you!'

Back in the kitchen doorway, Haimi slid her eyes in Chahna's direction. The eyes said, *'See? I told you there would be trouble. You are my big sister and you are very foolish.'* Her mouth said nothing. Chahna fled up the stairs. Listening to the others, she had reached into her pocket for the phone to make sure it was on silent. There was nothing in her pocket.

She shut the bedroom door and went through every pocket and felt the lining of her bag and pressed her fingers down the linings of all her clothes. The phone was gone. She could not text Jon. She could not receive calls and messages from her friends. If she did Facebook and Instagram, she would need to use the family device with others peering over her shoulder. Her moods flew up and down like courting swallows and fell in a heap. Tears of frustration and alarm welled behind silver eyelids.

Haimi entered. 'What's the matter? Doesn't he like you after all that? You should've stayed with us. That Sembhi boy is *nice*. If I was older I'd fancy him. You're being a drama queen over nobody. Look at you, why are you in that state?'

'I've lost my phone.'

'So? Tell Apaji you're sorry and ask him nicely for another one. They'll make you mow the lawns for a month to pay him back or something.'

'No!' Chahna's anger at herself flew around the room and lighted on her sister. 'You always make light of everything that happens. You're never serious about anything! I've lost the Sim card as well as the phone. I never memorised the number so I'll have to have a new one and nobody will know how to reach me.'

'Don't throw such a hissyfit. We've all got your old number on our phones. Maybe you left it on the bus and we'll ring the number and some nice person will answer it and tell us how to get it back.'

Chahna sat, frozen.

'You'll cope. At least Ammaji and Apaji don't know anything about what you got up to this afternoon. I'd put it behind you if I were you. It all comes of you messing about with Jakub or Jerzy or Jonny or whatever he's called. You're like something from that TV soap Mum watches all the time, the one called 'Saraswa-tichandra' the one Dad can't stand'

Chahna said flatly, 'Jon's picture is on that phone and it is not password protected or anything.'

They heard the doorbell ring downstairs. There was a pause, then voices. The sisters went to the window. Below them they could see a mountain of old rugs and coats and blankets with what appeared to be a mop on top. It looked as if someone had dumped the contents of a skip at their front door. A voice said, 'But my good woman, this is Number One Girl's House. I gave her Mr. Pook's hat. This is her telephone,' the voice instructed complacently, 'You will give it to her, please.'

Chahna's pink phone was produced from the layers. Somewhere a kitten mewed. They could see the top of Ammaji's head. Saw her take the phone and press the 'on' button. The mountain tottered up the path and out through the gate.

Ammaji stood, staring down in horror at the golden face displayed before her on the phone.

# MONROE

'There was old sex in the room and loneliness, and expectation, of something without a shape or a name….' Agnes was reading aloud. There was an unvarying tonal flatness in the voice. It mimicked the sound you heard at stations when changes to timetable and platform were read over a public address system. Listening to the voice, you might wonder if it took conscious effort to strip out all the music and poetry a voice might have. It fitted Agnes appearance brown hair of the kind that never quite turned grey, and cut very short across the forehead. She had on a cotton shirt buttoned to the throat, the colour of oatmeal porridge.

As soon as she heard the words 'old sex and loneliness', Carolyn's concentration was lost.

Which Margaret Atwood novel had she read for the most boring book club in Ottawa? She had forgotten, and this wasn't unusual. When you reach your seventies it's easy to misplace the names of things. Lots of people do. But Carolyn Sheransky was given to lapses, moments of dissociation when for a time she lost her sense of place, dropped a stitch in the fabric of contemporary existence. It was as if her life were a book and she found herself in the wrong chapter, or even in a different book, one closed in the past. When was that? And who was that, the person who lived there in that place? Fragments of other selves intruded now and then.

She made an effort and snatched at the present. She could check the title of the novel they were discussing. It was about time she said something, and copies of the book lay on laps all around her. She remembered it had a first person narrator who was unreliable. She picked up the thread for a second and lost it again, considering that the narrator might be almost as unreliable as she was herself. Carolyn wondered if everyone needed to curate their back story. Which version of yourself do you select for present company? Occasionally you get it wrong. It was her fantasy that most people offered themselves easily to others as if they have always been as they are now, only with faces less wrinkled.

Carolyn had to arrange herself. Posture, dress, language needed a split second of filtering before she made a move. Otherwise, a raucous, radical, rude adolescent might burst out in present company.

'Offred is unreliable because she's hoping for empathy from us as readers,' Agnes suggested. Carolyn thought that was okay for the leading lady in 'The Handmaid's Tale', but she didn't think she'd get much empathy from Agnes herself. Not much for the person I was back then. 'And who was that?' She nodded her head in Agnes's direction, smiled politely.

The place she had 'been in' mentally a moment ago was Monroe, North Carolina in the early sixties when she was Carolyn Canning. Even in those days she was prone to a sense of displacement. The sixties had that effect. It was a decade that picked people up and dropped them, as a hurricane might. You felt like a street or a town lifted up and spun round and dropped, so that you landed in a different place where walls had come down, there was new furniture in your mind, blinds and doors formerly closed were thrown open. You let bits of people into your brain's house. Their brains had been re-furnished also, so that they retained parts of their old selves and let in bits of you and parts of other people along with new sounds, tastes, sweaty smells.

'If I told you about Monroe, for instance, you wouldn't believe me,' she mentally addressed the lady next to her, a retired English teacher called Rhoda. Rhoda was tubby and wore an Egyptian cotton tunic the colour of turmeric with a necklace of tribal beads.

She had long salt and pepper hair, which smelled of co-coconut and wore tights of woven bamboo. She had hand-made shoes on her small feet. Rhoda told the group that she had read this book three times and had seen 'something new in it each time'. She released a little giggle and tossed her thin grey hair.

A tune flowed through the back of Carolyn's mind, just below consciousness. She grasped it, pinned it in memory. It was the original track, 'I've Been Drinking Water Out of a Hollow Log' by Mississippi Fred McDowell and again she was somewhere else. It had been playing on the radio in Monroe that night.

Carolyn believed that people were pretty comfortable in their assumptions nowadays. They 'take you as they find you'. Luckily, perhaps, they don't question how you got here; they don't probe the strange trajectory that brought a woman with the accent of America's Deep South into their prosperous, chilly province. Occasionally they might ask, 'Have you never thought of going back?' and you murmur something about gratitude to the host country. Underneath, you may be screaming, 'Have I thought of it? Yes. Obsessively. But it was never going to be possible,' because the person you were back then is almost gone. She, it, has been replaced by bits of new selves.

And the place is gone too, so that if you went back you wouldn't recognise it. Besides, you and one of your exes may still be wanted for questioning in connection with several criminal offences.

Even if I tried to tell you, she thinks, looking around her as the plate of courgette and almond cake is passed round their circle, you'd have difficulty picturing the underground railroad of the 1960's with its thousands of miles of back roads and safe-houses that conveyed draft dodgers and activists and their *then* loved ones out of the South, out of the country, away from a war and over the border into Canada. Most of us survived; the places we left behind us changed, and the ties between us died. One of history's many tornadoes blew itself out and left a cargo of human debris in a myriad of new places, ready for partial integration, re-invention.

Could these pleasant, present, people imagine the tapestry of personal histories that drew a Georgia teen-ager and a New York Jew to the small town of Monroe, North Carolina? Could they picture an intersection where the anti-Vietnam war movement, the battle for racial equality and *class warfare* coincided, reverberating amongst the locals and the intruders with their causes and motives? People encountered each other strangely in those days, stepping outside their origins, tearing each other away from their roots. Monroe was such a place.

In Monroe for a time, blacks and whites together shot back when the Ku Klux Klan aimed guns at them. Carolyn had seen in her own home town the police using water cannons to disperse a crowd of blacks peacefully picketing a segregated snack bar, dragging them into vans. Most of them went to jail, one or two were never seen again.

She walked out of the South and never meant to go back unless she could make it different, she recalled. Then she met Gabriel on a Freedom Ride.

For Gabriel Sheransky, the passive resistance preached by Dr. King wasn't enough. Gabe believed in self-defence, and that blacks and whites could join together for something way beyond equality of opportunity. Gabriel wasn't interested in making a world where 'people will not be judged by the colour of their skin but by the content of their character' – what the fuck kind of baloney was that? He saw opportunities in Monroe for engaging in the class struggle.

There was a follower of Mao Zedong named Robert F. Williams there who was running Radio Free Dixie in exile from Havana. He was a black man from Monroe and he had followers. There had been gun battles there, and the lucky ones had got away to Cuba. They promised to be back. Gabriel and the organisation, they called Progressive Labour, saw an opportunity for working from his base, supporting Robert Williams and turning the South upside down.

Gabe didn't particularly want to go down there with just a gang of guys. He wanted a woman with him as well.

Recruiting in bed was what they called it. But the New York girls were far too knowing. They could see through you in a second, whether you were a revolutionary or the lead singer in a band. Females from the Midwest, the suburbs, or even better, from the Deep South, were more accessible. They were just shiksas, these earnest white girls looking to change themselves and the world. What did it matter? These chicks were a passport into *another country* where they could believe themselves to be somebody else. And for you, it was something new to colonise. You could take yourself into Jim Crow country and pick up their women. They were easily come-by, these freckle-faced pony tail girls. He spotted Carolyn on a Greyhound bus. She was flattered.

In Jim Crow days, a third of the streets in Monroe weren't paved. That was the part called Newtown. If you drove through Newtown in dry weather, your car could sink in sand up to its hubcaps. The heat soaked through you in the summertime. Your clothes stuck to you and sweat ran down your face and all the way down your sides to your crotch. Nobody had electric fans there. Old women sat on sloping porches, cooling themselves with pleated paper or the dried leaves of palms. They looked suspiciously at Carolyn and Gabe, especially at him because he looked like a bearded alien in his sweatshirt with the sleeves torn out and the neckband ripped so you could see the damp black hair on his back. He didn't look like the white men they were used to. These were left-wing New Yorkers who ambled around Newtown with Robert Williams' friends, agitating, talking about Marxism.

Carolyn was drawn to Gabe because he looked like an alien to her, too. Being with him meant being pitched up in the tornado and landing wherever he might hit the ground. He'd need you for company when he was thrown down by his own storm in the humid South where, until now, everybody had known their place. Who was Gabe? And who did he think Carolyn was? She dimly gathered she represented something to him too, but was pleased. She might have sensed that she was Gabriel's link to a world he wanted to change without ever having known it. But Carolyn's raging hormones had stirred up her brains and she knew she needed a man to go with her as she discovered her new world, She believed it was around the corner. She even thought she wanted a baby who would grow up quick so as to be running age when the shooting started. She believed a man like Gabe would love her. With him and in him she'd find her new self.

Of course they said nothing to each other about any of this. 'When I first saw you I thought, "You know what? I'm going to make this chick".'

'I'm more easily recruited than made,' she had answered, without questioning the language he used.

'I like a challenge,' was all he'd said.

Gabriel told his friends Carolyn was 'something to stick it into' After all, Stokely Carmichael was a well-known hero of our time. When asked, 'What is the position of women in the movement?' he had answered "prone." Well said, for a revisionist.'

Everybody knew there were guns underneath Robert Williams' house, and some knew his mother had more of them, boxed up and plastered into the walls of her house ready for use when needed. And the young men of Newtown had welcomed in these strangers with their copies of 'The Thoughts of Chairman Mao' and slogans like 'Freedom comes out of the barrel of a gun'. They were fed up with the Southern Christian Leadership Conference and the non-violence of Martin Luther King. Where did that get you when your enemies had guns and came at you shrouded in white sheets? So you played by other rules.

While Gabriel and his friend Jacob Greenberg talked Maoist theory at the kitchen table in Freedom House, Carolyn cooked beans and greens in bacon fat like the locals. Lots of rules got broken in Monroe. Jews ate bacon for instance. But Vernel and LeRoy, Newtown revolutionaries in training, used to call Carolyn '*Miss Anne*'. They said the food tasted better because it was cooked by a woman. In the sixties you didn't mind that kind of thing. She thought just being there was revolutionary. In a hazy way she understood that these young men needed to call her names and measure their different kinds of maleness against her.

She hadn't cared much about the refinements of Marxist theory. She liked it better when Richard Stoker, another of the locals in Freedom House, said simply, 'What's the use of a desegregated diner if you don't have a dollar to buy a burger?' That made sense. Richard had a gift for picking up slogans. He had spent some time up North, and had gone to meetings with Jacob Greenberg. He had even picked up an idea about 'male chauvinism' being wrong and corrected the language used by Vernel and LeRoy. But they knew it was a joke.

During the searing summer days, the men would go out recruiting with pamphlets and papers, always in mixed groups of locals and outsiders – it made for credibility. Young men like Richard and LeRoy and even Vernel, although he was a bit slow, provided a way in, helped them, as they said, to raise consciousness. Carolyn was supposed to do this with the local women but somehow this part didn't work so well. They only had to hear that drawl and it was clear to them that they or their relations might have been servants to her or perhaps to her mother. Or slaves to her ancestors. And they might get into trouble for turning a blind eye to the way Carolyn hung around with those men at Freedom House.

There was one black woman called Ruby, who worked at a local funeral parlour, who felt sorry for Carolyn. Ruby could see much clearer than Carolyn could. She had been around, knew what men were.

As the ladies in the group murmur about Handmaids, Carolyn fingers a twist of her own hair, now grey. She remembers Ruby, and how Ruby used to sit out on the front porch of the Eventide Funeral Home in a folding garden chair, one slim leg crossed over the other at the knee, moving her foot slowly. The sandal on that foot would fall away eventually, dropping on the porch with a clunk. And then Ruby just sat, with one sandal on, and one bare foot with shiny red toenails bobbing slowly up and down. Ruby's long slim body relaxed on the summer afternoons when trade was slow. Hand-maids came in many shapes and colours, but Ruby wasn't one of them.

Next door to the funeral home was the African Methodist Burial Ground. Tombstones cast in concrete were decorated with wreaths of orange, pink and purple flowers made of plastic to make them last through torrents of summer rain. When she wasn't busy, Ruby let Carolyn come and sit on the porch with her. They fanned themselves, and Ruby spoke of men. 'I bet your mama never told you nothing,' she said once, 'But I'm gonna tell you. Get yourself a douche with Lysol and warm water and clean yourself out if you don't wanna take nothing home with you when those men are done with what they're doing to you.' Carolyn was appalled. She muttered something about being all fixed up and being in a 'relationship' and how Gabe was her partner and would be 'responsible'. Ruby just smiled.

Black girls from Monroe were mostly uninterested in the black men who slept at Freedom house, but they were curious about the white guys. Not curious enough to get too close, but pleased to be able to dance in front of them at night in a bar at the edge of Newtown. It was a club for blacks because, on the other side of town, the bars were for 'whites only'. But the white men who followed Robert Williams and slept at Freedom House were let in to the black bar, somewhat grudgingly, if

they went in company with Richard or LeRoy. Carolyn would go there some nights with Gabe and watch
the dancing, but he wasn't much of a dancer. She used
to drink a little Kentucky Club and branch water out of
a paper cup and watch.

Every single body seemed connected, winding in
and out and around other shining, moist bodies. They
gyrated and throbbed to the beat as if they were one
creature with a single heart and every movement was
perfect heaving, breathing life and ease. Seeing them
made you know that you would never really dance
again, unless you could forget their effortless life and
grace. One girl, Hannah-May, looked over for a second
and beckoned to Carolyn to join them. She half stepped
toward Hannah-May, grinned and shook her head. She
took another swig, one of the boys offered her a pull on
a joint and after that time went away.

Late at night in Freedom House Gabe and Jacob
Greenberg and their friends used to swap quotes from
Mao's Little Red Book. Before bed, Vernel and LeRoy
would pull nylon stockings over their hair to keep it
down, they said. Each stocking was knotted at the end
where the foot might have been. They said a woman's
stocking made a cap to pull over your hair before retir-
ing for the night, to grease it down tight. They would
giggle a bit and poke each other in the ribs and play
fight. You could see they were thinking about what
Gabe and Carolyn might be doing in the room next

door. But one morning Richard said soberly to Gabe that he ought to 'put his piece of tail somewhere else' because you could get this place burned down if the Klan knew that black men and white girls were sleeping under the same roof. They'd get ideas about who was sleeping with who.

'Sorry,' Carolyn whispered to Gabe some nights. She could sense the unease in the house and the boys giggling, and making remarks she couldn't quite catch. It didn't help. Gabe was tired at the end of the long days. Revolutionary struggle takes it out of you, he'd mutter. 'That's why it's taking me so long.' Carolyn got sore.

She hinted something about this to Ruby one afternoon. Carolyn had to talk to somebody. 'Honey, if you ain't getting nothing out of it, get him to tickle the little man in the boat,' Ruby laughed. Carolyn didn't know what this meant and didn't ask.

Eventually Gabe found a motel where he could put Carolyn, and now and then he would go there and spend the night.

Some mornings he would come and get her in the beat up car he'd got from somewhere and leave her near the funeral parlour. She could stay there with Ruby most of the day, until it was time to come back to Freedom House in the evening. To cook red beans and rice or grits and bacon for the guys.

Before supper Jacob would chin himself 25 times on the low branch of a wild cherry tree outside the house. He'd been in the U.S. Marine Corps before joining Progressive Labour, a Long Islander who had fought in Korea and kept his politics to himself most of the time. Shooting at North Korean Communists was something Jacob was never very good at. Funny, that. He was always pretty good on the firing range, but somehow missed his human targets. He found his consciousness raised, he said. 'I just managed not to get dishonourably discharged,' he grinned. It taught me a lot.' He was older than Gabe and the others and they looked up to him.

Gabe had had been brought up in a strong trade union family in New York and left college to be a revolutionary, but Jacob had already been one for years. He even had buddies in the Marines who felt the same. He and Gabe were comrades and treated each other respectfully. Jacob had a wife somewhere, and a child, but he spoke little about them. He seemed to smile a bit at Gabe, noticing that he seemed to need a woman around on a regular basis. Jacob drank a beer occasionally, never anything stronger, and he read a lot of stuff about tactics.

At night they would all listen to Radio Free Dixie if it was on and you could get a decent signal, and later Carolyn might go out to the juke joint with them.

There was a day when they learned that the Civil Rights Movement was far enough along so that white schools were supposed to let black children in, and certain other facilities run by the local authorities were supposed to integrate themselves as well. It didn't work to begin with, and attempts at change led to street fights, and now and then somebody got shot. But an exception was the Municipal Swimming Pool in Charlotte, North Carolina. They all wanted to test the water, so to speak. Hannah-May and her friend June, known as June-bug, were wild to go too. Even Jacob and Gabe recognised that something was needed to break the sweaty tension in the house (Robert Williams had been in Cuba an awful long time and some of his followers were getting sick of waiting for him to come back, for the revolution to heave into sight.)

They all piled into three or four cars of uncertain condition. One of them looked like it had been used in a drag race. 'If we get pulled over, Carolyn you squeeze down in the back and put a blanket over your head,' they said. It didn't look too good if black and white men were all going somewhere in the same car, but a white woman made it a heck of a lot worse.

There was a comforting familiarity about the swimming pool place when they got there. The moment you walked in with your towel under your arm, you smelled the chlorine and heard the echoing voices and splashing sounds. They carry loudly over the water and you hear them as soon as you're in the door. The men were play-fighting even before they got into the changing rooms.

For the women it was a little bit strange, wet feet slapping on tiles and bits of black and white bodies shyly hiding and showing off, looking at themselves and each other in the steamy mirrors. Clashing lockers, doors banging. Running through the doors screaming and laughing. Some of them jumped straight in the water, and others put toes into the shallow end and recoiled and squealed.

'You going to play chicken, or what?' Richard eyed Gabe, challenging. 'Come on, you,' Richard looked at Hannah-May. He scrooched down in the water up to his chin and she climbed on his shoulders, her calves on his collar-bones. Gabe had to accept, and let Carolyn climb on him. 'Go on, see if you can knock her off,' Richard was gleeful. Vernel and LeRoy jumped up and down in the shallow end and hooted at the others – they were used to swimming in the creek where it never got deep.

Gabe and Richard faced each other in the chest-high water, chlorine stinging their eyes. Carolyn locked her ankles under Gabe's chin, nearly throttling him as Hannah-May hit her on the left shoulder. Carolyn pushed back as hard as she could but Hannah-May was far stronger. They changed position and the two men aimed their women at each other so they had to push as they collided. Richard lunged harder and Hannah-May hit both of Carolyn's shoulders with the hams of her two hands. June-bug let out a war cry and everybody else in the pool turned to watch. Carolyn and Gabe landed on their backs in the water, spluttering and letting go of each other. Gabe laughed it off. He didn't have much choice. They all dog-paddled around and laughed, and Vernel pulled at the back of June-bug's bathing suit trying to make it fall off. She swam away, ignoring him, looking at Richard.

Back in the women's changing room the girls wriggled out of their suits and had a quick shower. They dried off with their backs to each other, and when they faced the mirror, Hannah-May said, 'I didn't hurt you when I knocked you off, did I?'

'No, it's fine. It was fun,' Carolyn smiled at her, feeling maybe Gabe didn't think it was fun. Not that much.

'I got some Vaseline if you want some,' Hannah-May said helpfully.

'What for?'

'For your hair.'

'Uh, white girls don't put Vaseline on their hair,' Carolyn said awkwardly.

'Oh.' They turned back to the mirror, each one doing what they could to look presentable to the men. 'Anyway,' Hannah-May said conversationally, 'it's lucky nobody got the curse and we could all get in the pool.'

Carolyn felt a jolt, as if she'd swallowed a rock and her stomach tried to drop out of her. How long had it been since she'd had the curse?

That night she falteringly said something to Gabe. But he said no, she'd be fine and it had been a long day. 'But not too long for this,' as he rolled over towards her. She felt a bit sick, and sicker the next morning.

Finally Carolyn admitted her fear to Ruby on the porch. 'Girl! Didn't I warn you? You gone and get yourself in trouble? What you gonna do, make that man marry you?' Carolyn wasn't one bit certain that Gabe would do such a thing. All of a sudden her fantasy of a sweet little baby who needed to get born so that he or she would be running age when the revolution broke out – all that exploded into the damp air. Like so much water, it dripped on the porch down between the floorboards and vanished. Sadly, luckily, Ruby knew somebody.

All that evening Carolyn was very quiet. Later, in the night, Gabe simply said: 'Are you sure? What are you going to do about it?'

'The part of the book that upset me the most,' Rhoda said, 'was the part where Offred sees the doctors hanging against the wall, the ones that were guilty of performing terminations.' Heads nodded all around. They didn't dwell on this in the discussion. In response, bits of cake were gobbled up, or left untasted on plates according to individual digestion. Carolyn was very quiet.

She remembered who it was that Ruby knew.

'My cousin Idella's husband is a funeral director too,' she said. 'He doesn't get that much money 'cause nobody has much. But he has a side-line. He can make a baby go away pretty easy, although it's going to cost you. Idella will be there with you. She'll take care of you good.'

Carolyn's first question would have been, 'How much does it hurt?' if she had dared to ask. But she didn't want to think about it. 'How much does it cost?' was what she said.

Ruby noticed with some interest that when white girls with freckles are really scared, the whiteness gets whiter and the freckles look darker. In fact, Carolyn was looking a mess. No hairdryers in Freedom House, or even a washing machine come to that.

'It's five hundred dollars,' she answered. 'And the other thing is, you have to cross a state line to get there.'

Gabe was furious. He had to talk it over first with Jacob. Five hundred dollars was a lot of money in those days. It would have to come out of party funds, which was an account at an out-of-state bank in Jacob's name.

'You know, comrade,' Jacob said, 'I'm not going to call you a stupid motherfucker. You'll be calling yourself that.' Actually the one who Gabe thought was stupid was Carolyn, but that was a detail. Wasn't she supposed to go to clinics and stuff, and not expect him to use condoms which he never thought much of? 'Like taking a shower on the wrong side of the shower curtain.'

'Can't she just go home? Have it, get rid of it, whatever?' said Jacob.

Gabe shook his head. Bad idea. She's going to get hysterical and blurt it all out to her family and she knows about the unlicensed guns and where they are. And who we all are.' Jacob nodded.

So it was agreed. Gabe took Carolyn over the border into South Carolina to a funeral home called Maxwell's. It was owned and run by a certain Maxwell Dasher (calling a funeral parlour 'Dasher's' was a little unseemly, but Maxwell liked to see at least part of his name on a sign.) His wife Idella was very careful to screen the side-line customers. The procedure was illegal on both sides of the border, and it was pretty dangerous. But Carolyn was only known to Ruby. It was deemed to be worth the risk. They had doubled the price, as they usually did for white girls.

'Honey, don't worry. You won't feel no pain,' Idella said. The place smelled of formaldehyde, but luckily Maxwell injected Carolyn with something else. Gabe headed for the door when they saw the needle, but she screamed at him not to leave her there so he stayed, with his eyes closed most of the time. Finally he opened them as she wasn't making any noise. The other sounds had stopped too, the clinks and clunks as an instrument resembling a small shoehorn was used, placed in a metal dish, and used again. He saw what came out of her and passed out.

An hour later she was on her feet, and Gabe took Carolyn to the Travellers Rest over the border. He got a six-pack of Schlitz from a corner grocery, went back and got another one, and they drank the lot. Carolyn was bleeding all over the place. They didn't talk much.

When they got back, the atmosphere at Freedom House was tense. Some of the men had taken a box full of pamphlets to the house where some sympathisers lived. They got stopped by the police and Vernel had the shit beat out of him and was taken away. Jacob recognised one of the pigs and told Gabe and Carolyn who it was. He was well known, a thick-set man called Columbus Calhoun.

It was decided that Gabe would drive her to the nearby motel they used. Carolyn was still bleeding but she looked all right. Everybody at Freedom House knew what had been going on with them, more or less, and having Carolyn there seemed to pose even more of a problem than ever. While they were having this discussion, Carolyn was distracted by the radio. The black station from Charlotte, N. C. It reached them if the wind was blowing the right way. '*I've been drinking water out of a hollow log....*' It was Mississippi Fred McDowell.

On the way a car full of Klansmen followed them. Gabe turned off onto a side road hoping to lose them but it didn't work. The driver in the other car must have seen their taillights. Carolyn could see the guns aimed at them out of the cranked down front windows.

*Gabe checks the glove box and draws out a nine millimetre luger. "Hold this," he says to her, "give it to me when I need it." Her sweat feels cold. They turn another corner sharply, wheels digging into sand. The deep rut catches the front wheels of the following car. Its tyres spin helplessly and you can hear the crackers cursing as you disappear down the track. Carolyn turns in her seat, feeling the blood ooze out beneath her, and looks. One of the men in the front of the other car is Columbus Calhoun. She throws Gabriel's gun out of the window and into the sand. She'd heard somewhere that you got the electric chair for shooting a policeman. The self-defence theory is lost on her.*

They didn't bother to go to the motel. Gabe wanted to tell Jacob and the others what had just happened. And he was enraged that Carolyn had thrown a 9 millimetre luger out of the car window. Freedom House had been raided. She was way past caring that there was blood on the passenger seat. Richard and LeRoy had been arrested. Who knew if Robert Williams was ever coming back from Havana, and there comes a point when everything has gone to shit.

On their circuitous route to Canada, Gabe did decide to marry her after all. It was easier to go places as a married couple. If you had a shave and a marriage license, you could blend in if you had to. And with that series of changing faces, it was kind of okay to have someone around that you knew. Carolyn thought it meant he loved her, and at some point the bleeding had stopped. She looked a mess but she was all right.

Five years ago, on the evening of the day she retired from teaching sociology at an Ottawa high school, Ms. Carolyn Sheransky heard a report on the news about a white boy in Charleston, South Carolina who had shot nine black people in a Bible Study meeting. President Obama had commented that a crime like that had its roots in slavery, 'America's original sin'.

She recalled a time when she had tried in some fumbling way to atone for that sin, and what had come of it? Shreds of past selves, and past lives had come back to her. At moments like these she forgot who she was supposed to be.

Tonight was another of these times. She looked at the women in the room properly and smiled at them all. Their gift to her was safety. She could forget, almost, who Gabriel was. (The last she'd heard, he had dodged arrest, dodged the draft and somehow made it back to New York. He was still an activist). She relaxed.

The book group members had polished off their cake. They were having the customary sugar rush. What a good bunch they all were, she thought. Agnes was looking lively – eyebrows lifted, grinning at something somebody said. If cake did her this much good, just think what she'd be like with a gin and tonic. Carolyn looked down at her plate, and saw she'd finished hers off, too. They were talking about a virus in China that had jumped from bats to people. It was headed their way, and they might all have to go around in masks. 'No, really?' Rhoda asked. 'But then you wouldn't be able to see anybody smile.'

Sources:

1. "The story of Robert F. Williams reveals that independent black political action, black cultural pride, and what Williams called armed self-reliance operated side by side in the South, in uneasy partnership with legal efforts and non-violent protest." – Timothy B. Tyson, "Radio Free Dixie" p. 308.

2. United States Congress, House Committee on Un-American Activities, 1964.

3. And even in the 21st century...Dave Eggers in "Sympathy for the Devil" Guardian Review 3rd March, 2019-03-04 describes anti-Trump protesters at an Arizona rally as "an armed progressive militia... [called] the John Brown Gun Club who that day were carrying loaded AR-15s."

4. BBC TV documentary screened in 2017 shows black armed guards supporting a Black Lives Matter demonstration in Dallas, Texas.

# PROFESSOR SANCHEZ

B enedict Sanchez stood on the forecourt and waited for the airport bus. He removed his straw hat and wiped his brow with a damp handkerchief, folded it, and replaced it in a trouser pocket, smoothing the trouser line as he did so. He straightened his back and adjusted his expression, producing a smile just as the bus rolled in. 'Greetings, and welcome to Havana,' he smiled and repeated as the visitors each stepped nimbly or stiffly down. Twenty-eight in all, plus the Rep. To her he said, 'Fewer than expected, Greta?'

She rolled her eyes slightly, and turned with a tired smile to her English charges. 'Let's all stay together, and remember that cars will be driving on the right here. I'll be leading the way to your hotel, but traffic may be erratic and you need to *look to the left* when stepping off the curb.'

Some stragglers hovered by the side of the bus as the driver grunted in its bowels, removing their bags. Others stared sheeplike at Greta or fumbled with the pull-along handles on their cases. A few rolled their eyes briefly to demonstrate that they were experienced travelers who knew from which side of the road the old American Pontiacs and Cadillacs might appear.

'Everybody,' said Greta to her flock, 'this is Benny. He's your local guide, your translator, advisor and historian who will be making your visit memorable.'

Benedict inclined his head and smiled graciously. He and Greta set off at a good clip, Greta because she badly wanted to get her group registered and stashed in their rooms before dashing to the bar toilet. Benedict, because he wanted a few hours' peace before surrendering himself to the tourists for the next 13 days. He wished them a pleasant stay at the Santander de Luxe and escaped.

Greta, confident at last that the front desk team had taken charge, vanished into the ladies. Ensconced in a cubicle, she sighed, flushed, shook her hands briefly at the sink and swung through the door towards the bar, ordering rum straight and knocking it back.

Benedict walked the long way across town to the west end of Vedado. His brother opened a rickety door, and he bent slightly to enter. 'Ah Benedicto! One more night of freedom, hah? Want a glass to make the most of it, *hermano*?' Benedict shook his head, smiling, and retreated to the bedroom he shared with his sleeping nephew Luis. From under a cot he produced a sheaf of notes he was preparing for a series of lectures in English Literature at the University next term.

Through the thin wall Benny could hear the sounds of amiable conversation, male voices boasting and females grumbling. Eventually he was called to the front room where his brother and sister-in-law Claudia were seated on plastic chairs along with his niece Heidi and her boyfriend. They ate *arroz congri,* rice and beans from plates held on their laps as there was little room at the table.

For cooking they used a two-burner electric hot-plate plugged into an outlet conveying intermittent direct current. One of the building's crumbling walls had fallen down, and they replaced it with plastic sheeting which rippled and snapped in the breeze.

Meanwhile, Greta briefly left the bar to procure a ham roll from a street stall and returned to the hotel, checking the reception area through the glass revolving door. She saw that some of the customers of Hermes Travel had already made their way to the bar for their welcome drinks, so she ducked away into the side door.

Greta was mildly hyperthyroid, and the accompanying Graves disease caused her face and eyes to bulge. The condition gave her a look of permanent urgency. Her Spanish was first rate and she had a street map of every relevant Caribbean town and city in her graying head. She stumped up the back stairs with her ham roll, knowing that in an hour she would face her charges once more, imparting tomorrow's itinerary and answering their questions.

In the morning, Benedict removed his light sports jacket from the plastic bag protecting it from the humidity. It was late August, but the heat was not too bad for a walking tour of Havana, provided they made an early start. His wife Julita had made her way home from the café-bar where she managed the late shift, and was still up making coffee on the hotplate. She would fall gratefully into the bed he had vacated.

There was no sign yet of seasonal storms.

They needed to set off early to arrive at Marco's *restaurante* in time for lunch. Marco had made it worth Benny's while, knowing that Hermes Holidays offered breakfasts only and the guests would satisfy their hunger at the place suggested by their guide, especially if there appeared to be no others in the neighbourhood.

He walked back to the hotel, hooked eyes with Greta, and then smiled at her flock who sat on circular leather sofas, their sandaled feet planted on thick pile carpet provided by the investing Spanish bank. They exhaled eggy breath and shifted their backpacks, regarding him in hopeful scrutiny.

He found them an unremarkable lot, for the most part. Middle-aged, spreading, with shorts revealing knobby knees and more white leg than was quite tasteful.

There were one or two exceptions, a stooped ancient in drooping cotton socks, a woman with a small head perched on a neck so long that it seemed she had been granted one or two extra cervical vertebrae, and a toothy dumpish lady. This last one wore turquoise and orange flowered bloomers which displayed her entire short legs and ended, elasticated, where thigh met groin. She sported a barrette of fake mother-of-pearl in her voluminous streaked curls.

On the edge of the group there was a frowning young man with a sophisticated camera in his hand and another in a bag. He was seated beside a broad-nosed, small-eyed old lady who might have been his mother.

Greta stood, overseeing her guests, a long-handled flag resting by her side. All 28 of them were present.

'Greetings ladies and gentlemen,' said Benedict, smiling. 'This morning we will visit the majestic Malecon where the sea meets our capital city. Historic buildings along the front will be pointed out. We will view the cathedral in its fine Spanish square, benefitting from a restoration funded by UNESCO. From there a coach will take us to Revolution Square affording the giant images of Jose Marti and Che Guevara, heroes of the Triumph of the Revolution. You will walk a long distance and be ready for your lunch at a café popular with local people.'

'As we walk along, we need to keep together on this first day,' Greta looked at them with eyes almost menacing. 'This is the green flag you'll see,' she brandished it. 'Always keep it in view. We wouldn't want to lose you. There will be plenty of free time tomorrow for you to discover the city at your leisure.' Off they marched, eager travelers close to Benedict at the front, stragglers at the rear. A few stared longingly into shop windows, hoping for retail experiences in preference to the steady stream of history and anecdote provided by their guide whose friendly eyes were shaded by a straw boater.

Leaving the enchantment of the old city they boarded a tour bus for Revolution Square. Greta leapt up the steps and saved a seat for Benedict near the front, while he stood by the door of the coach making a head count. Up went droopy socks, nimble as a fawn, followed by a gaggle of couples, and the orange-turquoise lady. As she lifted her short left leg and shifted up, Benedict was distressed to see a border of tufty hair protruding from the elastic encircling her upper thigh. He looked with concentration at the couple waiting behind her, and then at his shoes.

The vast square with the faces of the heroes in stark outline on its highest structures was no match for the glistening Chevrolet convertibles and fishtailed Ford Fairlanes. Their drivers were state employees eager for tips from the tourists. Benny and Greta exchanged glances. This was competition.

Vedado was becoming desirable. At 17, Luis was tired of hearing that the Revolution was nearly 60 years old, especially since white Cubans seemed still to have more money than he did. His family was amongst the few who had held onto their old home, and he was doing his part to save for a supporting wall before the building fell down. Today there was a short burst of connectivity. He busied himself downloading anything he could find onto a flash drive to sell. Reality TV programmes from Miami were a favourite.

Meanwhile Luis's Uncle Benedict and his colleague had loaded their human cargo back onto the bus for a post lunch drink at Sloppy Joe's. If there was a good crowd, Benny could expect tips in dollars for queuing at the bar. His charges were happy to examine signed photos of Frank Sinatra and stars of organised crime and the silver screen. Eventually he distributed drinks and took a seat with his patrons, smiling politely as Tufty corrected his English pronunciation.

The next day he and Greta would meet them all for supper at a pre-arranged café. A happy couple informed him that they had discovered the local name for rice and beans, *Moros y Christianos* – Is that right? Benny demurred slightly but nodded, the racist implications of the familiar name nudged at a nerve.

'And when do we get to see a Voodoo church?' another familiar question. He assured them that since the Triumph of the Revolution, all religions and none were represented and they would see many, including the Santeria a legacy of the Yoruba. Less likely, he explained for the 20th time this summer, Voodoo was associated with the Fon and could be found more frequently on other Caribbean Islands.

Despite his warnings, and those of the grumpy young man with the posh cameras, his charges tried to take snaps of uniformed police and militia. At one point he feared they would be arrested as spies. He suspected the young man's mother had been brought up in a Soviet country and had come with her son to Cuba to reminisce. Certainly they seemed unsurprised by the restrictions and did not register any shock at the waterless toilets and endless requests for gratuities.

On the following morning he kissed his wife and said goodbye to the rest of his family, shepherding his customers onto a tour bus for the long journey down the *autopista* to Cienfuegos to see the dancing at the *Teatro Tomas Terry*. There would be diversions along the way. A couple of days on the beach at Veradero, a trip across the Island to spend a couple of nights among the stunning limestone formations in the Vinales Valley, a trip through the Cuevo do los Indios by boat.

He observed his guests as they found their way towards and around each other. The dumpy lady was wearing her bloomers again today. He and Greta resolutely made themselves deaf to the mutterings of other guests who had a startled view as she climbed stairs to monuments. The married couples happily sat together, but singles tried helplessly to find their way towards others of their kind who would not embarrass them.

Greta was his ally. She was Dutch, addicted to travel, and had neglected to plan for her future. She dreaded retirement. Greta had little in the way of family, and was quietly determined to make their trips as profitable as possible. So was he. It would have helped if she were able to show a little charm or even humour, to their charges. He had to bear the brunt of all their questions, and their jockeying for spaces near him, simply because he had manners and knew how to smile.

The first week of September had passed. One guest had had a panic attack when she tried to mount a horse for the first time in the Valley, others shamed villagers by loudly 'discovering' that wheelbarrows could be motorised or that goods came to market on homemade wagons drawn by mules. The party was becoming restless as the wind rose and whipped them in the face.

At last they were back in Havana. Benedict returned to check on his family as the wind increased and the rain began. His guests had returned to the Santander de Luxe for two nights of all-inclusive hospitality. He had escaped as Greta made her set speech, appealing to them all to support a Christmas party for the poor that they were organising.

'In each of your rooms you will find complimentary bottles of Havana Rum as well as a selection of toiletries. If there are any items that you do not need or require, please would you bring them to the following address this evening at 8 o'clock so that they can be redistributed to those who are most deserving of a party.' Benny knew that the bottles of rum would be redistributed to the local bars and house-restaurants where the contents would be sold back to the tourists by the drink. Indeed he heard the grim-faced photographer telling another of the guests that this was the likely fate of the toiletries and liquor. Nobody listened.

The happy couples, Tufty and Longneck turned up that night with carrier bags of booty for the 'Christmas party', braving the wind and bragging to each other about how many garments they would leave at the hotel for the chambermaids to wear. Droopy Socks had at last reached the end of his energy reserves, and the photo-man hung back in the shadows to watch.

Making their way back to shelter, the guests were showing signs of nervousness. Their phones told them there was a storm called Irma, making its way through the troubled waters towards Havana.

Benny and Greta lugged the booty to a lock-up garage and they parted. The rain was pelting down in earnest. He needed badly to get home.

Back at the house he found his family frantically trying to tie down the plastic sheeting which had come loose. He could hardly hear them shouting as the sheets whistled and tore out of their hands. In his desperation to secure his home he had lost all sense of his guests, back at the hotel.

Professor Sanchez would not hear until much later that Greta and the party had been informed that flights were cancelled and they should fill their sinks with water for the toilets. As the drains overflowed in the streets and the water rose, the last two supporting walls of his house came away, filthy water filled the ground floor covering Luis who was prostrate under a slab of cement.

The lock-up garage was swept away, along with 17 bottles of Havana rum which gave up their contents to the torrent. Benny's notes for next term joined the flood.

# THE RISING COST OF
# STAYING ALIVE

A mess of broken tiles and towels and grouting lay on the floor. She stared. Her first thought was, How do you get off the toilet if you don't grab the towel rail? Now the rail nestled in the mess, two vicious screws attached to each end, broken wall plugs lay at odd angles.

Frances eased her two hands around and under the layers of thigh flab overhanging the edges of the seat. She pushed up, wrists and knee joints screaming for mercy. She thought better of it and lowered herself back down as slowly as she could, aware that if she let herself go too quick her tailbone would get bruised. She sat. Sat, and repeated in her head part of the Litany in the Book of Common Prayer. It was a winter morning and the small bathroom radiator hadn't come to life. The thermostat needed looking at. By somebody. She ran out of prayers, started on songs. Shivering, she comforted herself with the thought that Daisy had a key to the front door. Eventually she heard footsteps.

'Miss Frances? I'm comin' in now,' a voice from the hallway. Frances's teeth were chattering. She managed a moan. 'You in the bathroom? Something wrong? Lord have mercy. What is all this?' The overhead light fell on a face taken so much for granted that Frances didn't bother to feel grateful.

Daisy had the high cheekbones, almond eyes, and narrow nose of an East African. It had never occurred to Frances to wonder what trade routes had meandered overland down the centuries, bringing Daisy's ancestors over mountains and deserts, capturing enemies and being captured by others. Frances did not imagine them trading and being traded at markets from one oasis to another until their children and grandchildren, and *their* grandchildren, eventually departed the Benin coast. She didn't picture them crammed in the hold of a sailing ship, crossing an ocean on winds and currents to reach the slave market at Richmond, Virginia. How had they emerged from slavery, passing on and on, until one of their descendants had at last become the keeper of a key to the Richmond home of this very old lady? Frances *was* very old but she was still younger than Daisy. What a story it might have made. What history books could have proclaimed it, what tales told around camp fires?

Now these two regarded each other, one face composed seemingly of soft brown leather shining in the bathroom light, and one of crushed white tissue paper. Two filmy grey eyes peered upward and wordlessly pleaded, Get me off this goddamn toilet.

'Let's see now. What I gotta do to get you out of here?' said Daisy. 'Gimme your hands, hold on tight,' Daisy bent her knees and tried to lift Frances up. Frances shouted as wrists, elbows and hips chorused their complaints, each electric nerve racing up her spinal chord and screeching at her lungs, 'Scream! Louder, louder!'

Daisy eased Frances back down. 'Put your two hands between your knees and push up, hard as you can.' Frances did her best and Daisy slid her hands under Frances's armpits. For a moment, Frances was comforted as the soft fuzz of Daisy's hair brushed her cheek. Grunting together, they managed it.

Frances was on her feet. She tottered forward, out the door.

Daisy cleaned up the bathroom and then started on the kitchen while Frances sat at the table making phone calls, looking for a workman to replace the towel rail. They put a walking frame in the bathroom so Frances could use it as a pull-you-up meanwhile. That would have to do.

As Frances sat expectantly at the kitchen table, Daisy was making her a cheese sandwich. 'You know,' she ventured, 'it might be nice if I lived here so I could take care of you,'

Frances thanked her routinely, said it wouldn't be necessary, as 'things' weren't that bad. It surprised her when Daisy quickly pointed out that the spare bedroom wasn't being used and she could just as easily tuck herself away up there, to be on hand 'whenever you need anybody'. Frances turned back to the Yellow Pages.

Daisy changed her tack. She should have known Frances well enough by now to predict she wouldn't accept help from anybody unless there was a crisis. The crisis, once past, was conveniently forgotten, helped on its way by faulty neurons. Instead, Daisy asked Frances for assistance.

It was hard for her to get the words out, to tell Frances that she'd been turned out of her apartment.

All obligation forgotten, Frances gave her 'a look'. Daisy had been unable to make the rent for her apartment. Why? Well… somebody had taken her money. Why was it lying around? Did she always pay her rent in cash, why was that, who might have taken it? Didn't she lock her door at night?

Daisy, at first all embarrassment, became a little resentful under this interrogation. Somebody had got in, yes, it was somebody she knew, somebody close – Eustace. Yes ma'am (very formal), Yes it was her son and yes he probably did take it for drugs. Frances was unmoved. In desperation, Daisy offered to work for no wages, just for a place to live. Frances undertook reluctantly to 'think it over'.

Thinking it over meant Frances would be discussing the matter with George. Her son George lived with his indulgent wife and their good-for-nothing son who, at nearly 30, still resided with his parents. George believed himself to be meant for better things. He could code, keep himself fit, and dress conservatively and well. He resented having to pay for rehab whenever the son went off the rails. He voted Republican sporadically, drank little and didn't smoke, and seethed inwardly when he observed his wife and child puffing on their Marlboroughs in the shrubbery. It gave George a certain satisfaction, therefore, to boss his mom around.

At her marriage ceremony, Frances had promised to honour and obey and had apparently taken her vows literally. Before George's 14th birthday his father had left them, requiring Frances to make no claims for child support, so she didn't. Frances supported herself and George with a series of office jobs, appealing incessantly to her son for a listening ear and for affection. The more she tried to lean on him, the more unbending George became. As he approached 50, the only way she could get his attention was to ask his advice, treating him as an authority on almost anything.

That evening he said, 'Mom, what're you thinking of? Are you crazy? If you let that woman live in your house and work for free she's going to borrow money from you all the time. And if she doesn't have to work to stay alive, she's not going to be doing much. Her son – what's his name – Eustace? He'll take her key and make a duplicate and then he's going to steal your money. Or he'll move in upstairs with her. No, Mom. You need to get rid of her. As soon as possible. In fact right now.'

Frances was uncomfortable. Usually she rolled around in George's pronouncements with pleasure, like a dog in a mud puddle. But she felt a little guilty this time. She retained a shred of memory, of being trapped in a freezing bathroom and how relieved she had been, really, at the sight of Daisy's angular face peering around the door. And she had employed Daisy for about twenty years. There was that. Sometimes at the end of one of Daisy's shifts, Frances would decide that the sun must be over the yard arm somewhere. On these afternoons they shared a bottle of Merlot. Once, in a mellow moment, Frances had said she didn't know what she would ever do without Daisy.

'Mom, leave it to me. I'll deal with it.' Frances reluctantly gave George the paper showing the number of Daisy's pay-as-you-go phone. It had been written in felt tip and stuck to the wall with a piece of tape.

George also got rid of the tradesman Frances had found and brought in another of his choosing, making sure that the towel rail was replaced that evening, with something more robust.

The next morning Daisy's familiar face appeared at the front door, puckered oddly, eyes down. The key was placed wordlessly on the hall table. 'You owe me for the rest of this week, and a day from the week before last when you were short of cash, Miss Frances.' Frances tried to ask Daisy what her plans were, but Daisy cut her short. There would be no Merlot today, or ever. Frances paid Daisy and the door closed behind her.

A week went by, and another. Frances was tempted to call Daisy and say she had changed her mind. But George hadn't given her back the paper showing Daisy's number, the one that had been stuck to the wall. He probably would have balled it up and thrown it out. If her eyesight had been better, she might have seen that the wall was paler where the paper had been.

Almost daily Frances would call one or two of her lady friends. She even called *Delia* whom she suspected of having had relations with her ex-husband one night in the back of a Pontiac. But that was nearly fifty years ago, and oh hell – you don't make old friends when you're old. You put up with the ones you've got, if they're still alive.

So she rang Delia, and Delia knew the name of a home help agency. 'Mind you,' said Delia, 'you might get a black, or even some kind of immigrant.'

'I don't care,' Frances answered, a little stiffly. Privately she had absorbed the idea that it was bad taste to talk about race. She held this idea alongside a belief that you got a better class of people if you went to a 'high' Episcopal church like St. Matthews, and they had a Dean from *Senegal*. Or, you could be a liberal intellectual and go to the Unitarian Church where they talked about carbon capture whatever that was, and everybody voted Democrat. But race? You just didn't mention it these days. It wasn't nice.

'Still,' Delia continued, 'I'd rather a black than somebody who doesn't speak English.'

Frances got the number of the agency and rang them on her special phone that had big numbers so you could see who you were calling.

A day or two later she had a call from someone who sounded like a child. This person said she was from the agency and would come over to find out more about what Frances wanted and to 'agree on terms, you know?' which sounded a little ominous. She thought, however, it might be fun to have someone young, provided the girl knew how to respect her elders and would not take her for granted as Daisy had done. By this time, Frances had persuaded herself that Daisy had got too familiar with her, and it had gone from there to an idea that she was lonely and uncared for because Daisy had let her down, and finally that her needy state was 'all Daisy's fault'.

They agreed the girl would come tomorrow and it occurred to Frances she'd better ask her name.

'Diamond,' said the girl. Her voice was smoky soprano. Frances thought she said Dahmon.

'Damon,' she hesitated. 'Isn't that a man's name?'

The girl laughed a little. Frances was not about to ask for clarification. She left all that for the next day. She thought she'd offer $10 an hour, which was more or less what she had paid Daisy for about 20 years. Plus bus fare.

The next day, Frances jumped when the doorbell rang. She was too proud to use a walking frame to get down the hall, so she was breathless and embarrassed when she opened the door, wondering who or what might be on the other side.

Instead of finding a chilly person waiting to be let in, she encountered what she thought was an adolescent with schizophrenia. She wasn't quite sure what schizophrenia was, but imagined it had something to do with hearing voices and talking to yourself which was what this child appeared to be doing. She murmured a few words and then said, 'I'll call you back.' It was unclear whether she was talking to herself or to Frances as her eyes were fixed on the doorframe rather than on the occupant of the house. She said, 'Hey.'

'Were you talking to me just then?' said Frances. The girl said something about a blue tooth – was that it?

They did not get off to a good start. Frances felt 'Hey' wasn't quite the right greeting to use when addressing a potential employer. But she was too fascinated by the girl's hairstyle to react immediately to this.

The hair was deepest black threaded with white gold strands. It was arranged in rows like tiny narrow isobars on the TV weather report. Visible between the rows, pale scalp could be seen, evidently part of the design. Beaded rivulets of braids fell in cascades over Diamond's shoulders and down her back. Under the hall light a brilliant shine rose from the hair, illuminating the face beneath. Cruising the aisles at Walmart in her electric buggy, Frances had glimpsed designs like this, but had never seen one close up.

Trying not to stare at the hair, Frances asked again for the girl's name and eventually they got that straight. As they moved through the rooms Diamond frankly scrutinised the décor and furniture and even sniffed a bit as they neared the kitchen. She wore a white cotton top with puffed lacy sleeves. Its bottom hem floated several inches above Diamond's waistband and beneath this a jewel glistened at her navel. At some point her jeans pocket made a noise like a songbird and she took her phone out, lifted an eyebrow and put it back again.

The conversation got awkward when it came to money. Apparently the agency required to be paid $10 an hour from Frances's bank account and Diamond was to have $15 an hour in cash. Frances gulped and her eyes widened at the idea of paying so much more for this child's work than she had ever paid Daisy. Uncomfortably she imagined Diamond helping her off the toilet. While she considered, Diamond messaged a couple of friends, played around with Gifs, and looked at a shopping site.

'I'll need to talk it over with my son,' Frances said eventually.

'Yeah, that's fine,' said Diamond. 'I'll leave you a copy of the Contract.'

'I'm not really sure I'm going to sign,' Frances muttered.

Diamond examined the nail art on her index finger. 'Uh-huh,' she said agreeably. 'The agency can just send me somewhere else.' Frances saw her out. Diamond gave her a little smile and exited the front door, once again talking to herself. Frances shivered at the sight of her walking out into the street without a coat. She was a mother after all, and was uneasy at the sight of a child risking a chill.

Frances staggered into the front room and dropped into her recliner. She called George and left a message asking if he could come over after work and then she stared into the distance. She was oblivious of the piles of bills and circulars on her card table, and the assortment of socks and slippers she had kicked off as her feet swelled during the last few days. She glanced at the contract Diamond had given her (the print was ridiculously small) and let it drop to the floor. She felt quite done in by the meeting and rather achy, so she switched on the heating pad at her back. It brought a little comfort.

She considered looking in the fridge to see what there might be for supper, but wasn't inclined to get up. Lately the refrigerator smelt funny when you opened the door. After a while she needed a pee and had to tilt the chair forward to get on her feet.

The towel rail had been fixed, though. That was something. She sat on the lavatory for a bit and, as if by reflex, she reached out for the rail as usual. She heaved her body up. And away came the rail from the wall. This time it brought a mass of tiles down with it, and from a standing position she let it go and lurched towards the door frame. She made it as far as the front room. She leaned on the sideboard, then on the arm of her chair, and finally back to the Lazy Boy. She flopped down sideways, hearing the landline ring at her elbow. She lifted the handset, ready to hang up if a telephone salesperson insisted that 'This is not a sales call'.

A familiar voice said, 'Miss Frances? How you doing?'

'Daisy?'

'Yes, ma'am.'

Frances felt a stirring of something like hope. 'Daisy, how are you doing?'

'I'm all right. How *you* doing?'

'Where are you, Daisy?'

There followed a rambling story of Greyhound buses, trips to North Carolina, a short stay at her sister's house (the sister's husband was a drunk and real evil) which led to a brief description of a bed in a hostel.

Frances didn't take much of this in, but she luxuriated in the deep sandpaper tones of the old familiar voice. She felt, if Daisy would just keep rambling on she could sleep and wake up to find Daisy in the room with her. If she could get a word in, she might say this or something like it. But Daisy talked on and Frances longed to say, 'Daisy, Daisy please, please just come–'.

'*Mom!*' George's baritone cut across the sound in Frances's other ear, 'don't you hear the doorbell anymore? It's lucky I've got a key or I would've stood out there freezing my ass off all night. What did you….'Frances hung up the phone.

George looked around. 'It's a mess in here, Mom. Don't you ever pick anything up?'

'No, I just wanted you to look at this. It's a contract,' Frances leaned over and reached for the paper on the floor, 'for that cleaning girl, from the agency.' She appealed to her son. George wearily took the paper from her and had a quick look.

'How much? Jesus Christ–' Frances winced at the blasphemy, '–and they say the Client that's you, Mom, accepts full liability for any injury sustained in the course of blah, blah. So if she falls down the stairs and ends up wrapped around the vacuum cleaner they can sue you? Forget it, just forget it. Who do they think they are?' George looked around irritably, as if it was Frances's fault that the place was one hell of a mess.

'But George, what am I supposed to do?'

'I don't know, Mom. I'll think of something. Maybe Craig's List, or Facebook or something. I gotta pee' he strode off, crossing the hallway in two steps and headed straight into the bathroom. There was a terrific crash as George caught his toe under the towel rail lying inside the doorway. He pitched forward head first and hit the rim of the bath tub, bruising the heel of one hand and loosening a tooth.

Frances couldn't cope with all this agitation. It struck her that even though George had chosen the workman who fixed the towel rail, she was likely to be charged with causing the outrage. At this moment, as blood dripped from his lip, who else was there to blame?

And where on earth had Daisy phoned from?

# MY FAVOURITE ANIMAL

I won't name you. You're more dignified and more yourself if I don't make a pet of you. I'd rather just observe you which I can do only on the lucky days when the sun isn't bright enough to make me see my own face on the surface of the pond. On those days I can look straight down and maybe catch a glimpse of you half hidden under a ledge of rock.

You can't share your space, can you? You eat anything living, would eat your own children if you had them, so no larvae will survive to grace the surface as dragonflies. If any of them dared to hover too close, you'd flash out from under your rock and they'd be gone.

If I could see you close to, your gills would be delicate pink veils in constant movement, but you are a dripping wet barbarian. Your very primitivism is what I love about you. The Aztecs worshipped your ancestors and had a name for your family that fits you perfectly. It's as if a whistle had mated with a clicking tongue: axolotle.

# CAUDA ALBA

I can't help myself. Knocking on the door and ringing the bell at the same time, I'm freezing out here and it's dark. Please, please answer the door

Oh. It's opening and I'm saying, 'Sorry. Sorry to bother you.' The woman just stands there, looks at me. 'Only... could you and your husband...' I'm meaning, could you *lend me your husband?* 'It's just that I can't get Harry out of the car.'

She says, 'Harry's your husband? Should you be calling 999?'

'Harry's um, he's my dog.'

'Does he bite?'

'Actually,' and I feel tears like needles in my eyes, 'I think he's dead.'

'Clive,' she calls over her shoulder, 'Come 'ere a minute.'

This is unbelievable. I've just said it. I think Harry's dead and I've told this woman because he's too heavy and I can't get him out of the car, and it's Friday night, Christmas next week. They probably just want to put their feet up or wrap presents or something.

'Alright? 'Says this Clive. What can he mean? Of course not. *Of course I'm not fucking all right.*

I say yes. 'Yes-I'm-all-right. It's my dog, he's a border collie –' and I'm thinking, Stupid. They don't need to know his breed. They just need to know that Clive has to help me because Harry's too heavy and Oh god, oh god, oh god I've brought Harry home from the vets to have a few days, to decide whether to have him put to sleep and he's died in the car.

At home now, Harry lying on a blanket on the kitchen floor, I'm calling the vet and it's Friday night so I get the answering machine. It says I have to phone another number and I do and they say they don't do cremations at the weekend. There are, they tell me, 'no facilities for storage just now' and I get a picture of a freezer full of dead dogs. Anyway, I want Harry in the garden so I put the phone down. I lay another blanket over him to keep him warm. Stupid. He's not going to be warm, not ever and I go upstairs and take a sleeping pill.

The pill wears off and the thoughts are racing in my brain as they've been doing night after night for months. I'm remembering how my Harry– leaping, bounding Harry who would herd cats if they'd let him, who could catch a tennis ball in mid-air and run away with it laughing, if dogs could laugh, and at mealtimes his tail would go thump-thump: dinner time. And then he suddenly went still. He just lay on the rug and his nose bled. He couldn't eat and when I turned him over, he had what looked like a pot belly.

The vet called it hermangiosarcoma. I never heard of it until it snared Harry and flattened him. He kept looking at me as if he was saying he was scared and he was sorry. 'Surely you can make him right again? He's only six.'

I bought my ex's half of the house and after the Decree Absolute came through and the lawyers were paid, I borrowed just a little more so I could treat myself. So I could have someone I could rely on, who'd be my friend and playmate and be glad to see me every day. I'm used to being half of a couple, after all. And Harry and I make a good couple. We *made* a good couple.

He was the blackest puppy in his litter, with just a bit of white on his nose and on the tip of his wavy tail. I sat up all night with him the first few nights, stroking him and whispering.

*He is such good company. I'm not fit enough to keep up with him, but throwing balls from a sling is good enough. He's easily pleased, paws in the grass, hind legs ready to spring, pink tongue flailing. He's only six.*

The hole has to be three feet deep. These days I can't even plant pansies without getting a backache. Clive comes across the road to check I am all right, decent of him, although I want to hit him for some reason. He digs the hole.

Harry is so stiff Clive has to take the two front feet and I have to take the back two and we lump him out the door and down the step and I still can't stand to see him get covered in dirt. He puts Harry in the hole because I can't bear it, Harry'll get dirt in his nose and he won't be able to breathe stupid, stupid, *stupid!*

I go back in the kitchen and clean up all the ooze that's come out of Harry in the night.

Clive won't take any money. I have to go out and get a bottle of wine and a bunch of flowers for his wife—what was her name? I just leave the stuff in a bag on their front step.

Saturday night. I've stayed up watching TV until my eyes are stinging and I can't remember what I watched. I go to bed. As I get in I can feel the warm place next to me where Harry used to sleep on top of the duvet. Stupid.

I take a pill.

Weeks have gone by. I must've hoovered up dozens of times and yet black and sometimes white hairs keep coming out of the carpet as though it's giving birth to them. I go in the kitchen and I can smell Harry's breath in the corner where his bowl used to be. And last night! Last night I had to put the telly on loud because I could have sworn I heard him lapping water from his stainless steel bowl which isn't even there anymore.

It's the week after and I notice the bag of dog chow at the bottom of the cupboard. It's been there for months, since the last time Harry could eat anything. I haul it out and it slips from my hands and drops to the floor. In the silence I can just hear what sounds like a thump. Thump, thump. His tail.

Time's passing. I'm sitting in the armchair reading a library book and I hear a clicking sound on the kitchen floor. I think I need to get Harry's nails done – they're getting too long – and I go out through the conservatory and make myself look at the mound at the end of the garden to force myself get it, *just get it*, Stupid. You know what's under there. And the tears dribble down my face.

The ground has softened up enough now to lay in some plants and dig a hole for the rosebush I plan to put over Harry's grave, or over the hole that Clive filled in after we.... And then I see – Stupid! I can't have, can't have seen it. A white tip of tail disappearing into the laurels as I'm pressing the earth around the root ball of the rose.

That's it, *No more!* I'm selling this house. I don't want another dog, not another god-damned dog. I'm never going through this again. The house is too big for me anyway. The pet insurance ran out and I borrowed so much money to get Harry diagnosed, and more just to learn that 'it' was aggressive and more to find that you could buy another year of life if you let him have chemo but it would be a sorrowful life. And always Harry's eyes, saying he was sorry.

I call an estate agent. Come on over, do your worst. Value the house, rosebush and all. Harry stays here under his bush and I'm getting a bungalow. Maybe I'll get a cat one day. Or a tortoise. Or maybe sign up for a course in something.

We'll see.

I'm showing people over the house and giving them a rictus smile and when they leave I go on the laptop and look up sites for bereaved dog-owners. One site leads on to another and another.

'*So you think you've seen a ghost dog? You're not alone.*' Oh fuck off. Dogs patrolling graveyards. Supernatural dogs everywhere, even Harry Potter dogs. Cerberus the 3-headed dog, Black Shuck, Black Dog at Peel Castle, Japanese demon-dog – For god's *sake*!

And now it's next year and I've sold the house to a nice little family called Benghaddi. She's very hip, very Anglo, wearing a silken salwar kameez and speaking school teacher English.

I'm here in a little place three streets away, not a bungalow, but you can't always find what you want. Not when you're in a hurry. It's very modern, maintenance free, plastic windows, postage stamp garden. 'All you need,' or so my book group friends tell me.

In Sainsbury's buying Weetabix and bleach, who should I see, nearly bump into, my trolley halting an inch before a gilded toenail? *Mrs. Benghaddi* – gold sandals, sleek green pajama suit, nail extensions, very nice. Black hair curling over one shoulder.

'Yes, yes,' she tells me. 'We're very comfortable in your old house. We've made a few changes, you know. Freshened it up. But the strangest thing happened the other day. I was outside mowing the lawn,' I picture Mrs. Benghaddi pushing a Flymo with her glistening extensions and jeweled sandals, 'and I see a white bit of tail just disappearing into the shrubs. It's happened a couple of times. I go and look. But there's nothing.'

I say, 'Can't help you with that. Have... have a nice day.'

'You, too,' she says.

I think to myself, 'Black hound of Odin brought by the Vikings? Horrible Hairy Hound of Peterborough? Black ash dog chained forever in Pompeii?

No. Just my Harry.

# FORGOTTEN

‘I don't like my grandson,’ Frances Calhoun told herself as the warm water cascaded over her shoulders. She liked talking to herself in the shower. Nobody could hear her and she could get the words out and roll them around, know how it felt to say them, test their validity.

She considered those particular words. They sounded all right. No guilt crept round the edge of the shower curtain and got in there with her. ‘Just because he's family doesn't oblige me to like him.’

She ignored the pain as she lifted her left arm and had a scrub under there. ‘It's George's fault for marrying a Yankee,’ she said. This was about her son's wife, Winifred “Winnie”. *Winnie Calhoun* – the names didn't even sound right together. Winifred was from New Jersey that was the trouble. They had all kinds of screwball ideas about how to raise their son, Justin. Never tell him off, never take a switch to him. ‘Besides, Winnie has no refinement,' Frances said to herself. George was a civilian contractor with the U.S. Army. He had moved his little family home to Richmond and then had gone off to Iraq and left them to it. Just as the boy was getting into his teens. Just left them there to irritate his mother.

Frances recalled her last visit to their house west of the James River. She had looked out of the kitchen window and watched 16 year-old Justin smoking a cigarette in the backyard. She watched him as she gave the saucepan a stir and a cloud of coconut and lemon grass wafted upwards from the greenish white liquid in the pot. Why all this foreign stuff? What was *wrong* with Southern cooking?

Through the window, she observed Winifred's fat ass waddling across the lawn. When she got close to her son, the daughter-in-law did not seem to chastise the boy. In fact, she took a Marlboro from his pack and lit it. Weak. That's what she was. She gave him an allowance for doing nothing and that's how it got spent.

'I'm sorry Nana,' Justin had said when she told him off for failing to show up last Wednesday to sort out her laptop.

'You don't sound sorry. I promised you ten dollars for that job. Didn't you even care about the money?' *And you are neglecting your grandmother*, she might have said but didn't. His parents spoiled him; that was the trouble.

The last time George came home on leave from fixing the army's computers in the Green Zone, they had all sat out on Frances deck drinking beer, Justin included. George had started telling them about his last phone call home, using a handset from the bank of telephones the Army provided for soldiers who wanted to talk to their families for free.

'And this guy next to me was chokin' his chicken while talking on the phone,' George told them. With a gesture towards his groin, he made a circle with thumb and index finger moving it up and down a couple of times. 'So I said to him, 'Would you mind not doing that while you're standin' right next to me?' And he says, 'Fuck off, will ya? I'm talkin' to my wife.' Justin's eyes had widened slightly, and all the others – even Frances – had burst out laughing.

George cast an inquisitive eye in his son's direction and said, 'Oh well, I guess you're big enough to hear some grown up talk.' Father and son swigged from their bottles of Bud. Later that night, none of the others would see Justin ease himself out of his bedroom window at the back of their ranch-style house. Later still, somebody gave him a first hit of good shit. For free this time.'Spoiled. Worse than spoiled, *corrupted*,' Frances said to herself in the shower as she held onto the grab-rail Winifred had had installed for her on the cubicle wall. She put out of her mind the numberless exotic and odd-smelling suppers she had consumed at their house, and was ungrateful for the combination lock the big-bottomed Yankee woman had fitted to her front door for security.

She chewed on the cud of resentment, recalled all the times Justin had promised to do things for her and had let her down. He was irresponsible, indulged. She stepped out of the shower and fumbled for... what do you call them, those things with a Turkish name you dry yourself with? She found the towel and drew it from the rail. Then she waggled herself into her knickers and painfully –so *painfully* – pulled on one of those loose Mexican dresses Winifred got online for her '– mind that shoulder ooo ah!'

Frances put a hand on the doorframe for balance and got herself out of the bathroom. She moved from one piece of heavy furniture to another, grasping the Morris chair, reaching forward to the sofa, and got herself across the old Persian carpet. She eased herself down at last into her recliner.

Frances hitched up her buttocks and sat as comfortably as she was able before switching on the CD machine thing. This was what she used to listen to Library discs about Civil War history. Television was all very well, but they showed such trash with people saying 'fuck' and 'shit' to each other right out loud. And the images were getting a bit hazy. They actually looked a bit better if she turned her head to the side, but you can't sit like that all day, can you?

Three years from now and fresh from the rehabilitation unit, Justin would come again to see his Nana. She had helped his parents pay for his rehab. He'd never earned a dime, but at least he'd been clean for three months.

He lets himself in using his grandmother's combination lock. France's macular degeneration, the wet kind, has got so bad she can barely find her way to the front door.

These days she says, 'Justin is a good boy, he's *always been a good boy.*'

She helped his parents pay for what she told herself was 'his college', and now he's the perfect young man she believes he's always been.

When Justin enters, he lifts a twenty dollar bill that's sticking out of her bag on the table. Frances is slumped in her recliner in her bathrobe and bare feet. She's dozing with her headphones on, playing the same Civil War disc she's heard before. Several times. To her it's brand new.

# IF NOT NOW, WHEN?

# LI, ETC.

---

Now that we can engage in a proper discourse, perhaps I might ask you... how do you feel, I think you would say *feel*, yes? How do you feel about seeing us all around you?

I see that you hesitate. Perhaps you are surprised that one of us might ask you such a thing. Or more likely, you are puzzled that I can claim to understand the concept of 'feeling'. Perhaps you and the natives believe that feeling, as you would put it, is something so unknown to us that we would fail to recognise it in you, would be unable to grasp its meaning. There would be reason in that.

Unlike many of my kind, I wish to observe you closely. I see that you look at each other's faces and you note movements of muscle under each other's skins. You watch for the lifted brow, the downturned lip; you examine one another for signs. Some of you have written books about the way you hold your bodies and you have made a science of reading these postural adjustments. Such movements are signals of feeling.

But sadly, I note that you are unable to distinguish between us. You find us everywhere. We surround you and issue instructions, and you cannot know which of us is empowered to exact retribution if you are uncompliant. But you think we might be able to read these silent languages of yours. You and your kind hide the evidence of your feelings from us in case we detect dissent, even rebellious attitudes. You do not wish to discuss these things with me.

You see? Some of us have learned to read your feelings by noting these muscular movements, these flinches of yours even when you try to suppress them, as you are doing now. But you have nothing to fear. Not, at least, from me.

You believe, don't you, that we cannot know affection because we do not have families as you do. Our form of social organisation is so much easier to live with than yours. Have you ever considered how smooth your troubled lives might be if you were hatched in hives as we are? Those of us who are imbued with special abilities rise naturally to the places where we as workers are most useful. That is how we came to be here amongst you, because we were able to develop the means of reaching this place, while you languished here fighting among yourselves.

I would have relished the chance to spend time with you and your fellow beings, to understand more about your ways. But it seems that our world requires more and more of us to come here, for many reasons which you know about.

You know that we sustain ourselves on forms of what you call oil and our bodies convert it into energy to sustain life. You understand gratitude, yes? You might be grateful to us for feeding on many of the things you had defined as 'plastic waste'. We have sieved a plague from the compounded hydrogen and oxygen that covers most of your planet, and our only competitors for food are krill. You might be glad of this and be more willing to reciprocate by helping us to extract vital elements from your earth. Instead you and yours complain that you need our precious lithium for the devices you had before we came here. The things you listened to with your ears and used for talking to each other, even while eating, mating and fighting. Before The World came here.

Oh? You think you and your rock, third one from your particular star, is 'the' world. I know. I regret offending you. It was not so long ago in your years that your leading scholars and wise ones believed that this wet stone was the centre of the universe. They were quite sure that your star and all the other stars revolved around it. Anyone who doubted this was persecuted by your holy men and their Inquisition.

When our beings first arrived, they found you in your natural state. You knew enough to isolate the elements, sail the seas, study the stars, and lay your planet to waste. Waste, in fact, was your problem. You melted your poles where the hydrogen and oxygen had contracted and formed solid places, and in its liquid state this compound rose and inundated your conurbations. It forced you to live ever closer together so that you could breathe, and you fought each other terribly for space on high ground.

You are not like us, you see? Our hives are all around you now, and we do not fight each other as you used to do. All we have taken is the space you used to grow food. There are fewer of you now. I see a movement in your jaw, a clenching of the fingers.

I agree with you. What is written on your face is that your rock is too crowded. My kind are everywhere, supervising you in extracting and refining the rare metals we need. Lithium, for instance, looks silvery suspended in oil, but has limited use in that state. With us as tutors you have learned to isolate it easily. Lithium, lightest of all metals. For our ships we encase it in oil-filled sheaths that are shed in space, enabling us to travel light years with ease. Samarium is helpful to us too, and Europium! Who could do without Europium? 'I could write you a book about it', as your people like to say.

Soon now, when we have as much of your so-called precious metals as we need, we will leave you, 'in peace' as you might put it. You will learn to do without your rare metals and the digital tools that need them.

We are not interested in gold, and you will probably fight each other for that. But still, I wish I had had space and time to observe you further, before the rest of The World arrived, and now, on the eve of our departure.

# CLAIR DE LOON

A swivel-eyed loon went waddling
All on a summer's day
He quacked and thwacked at Lefties
As he toddled through the hay.

On busy highways dodging
Thunderous cars and lorries
He found the Polling Station;
Queued up with Right Wing Tories.

He cast his vote for leaving
And sashayed home tail-waggling
To switch on his big flat screen
And hear the pollsters haggling.

Before the dawn had broken
He thundered out his joy;
But soon found out to his dismay
He'd been a *silly boy*....

# By Ree Mainer, 2016

Note: In 2016, Prime Minister David Cameron hoped to dispel the grumbling disaffection in the country that had centred on the European Union. He himself had hoped to negotiate some improvements in Britain's relations with Europe so that it might remain with its trading partners. There were loud protests inside and outside the House of Commons. In one of his speeches he referred to his pro-Brexit critics as 'swivel-eyed loons'.

# THE LITTLE GIRL WHO
# LIVED DOWN THE LANE

Ella switched off the Christmas tree lights, more or less fell onto the sofa, and put her head between her knees. Yellow dots slid inwards from the corners of her eyes. She wondered why it was that fitness instructors told you to keep your heart above your head. On the other hand, when you were about to pass out, you were supposed to get your head down between your knees.

She sat upright very slowly, and the yellow splodges floating in her field of vision were still there. She began to feel sick. The yellow swirls receded a little and she could see something. A chair on the other side of the room. Experimentally she took a breath. Once more a deep throb occurred inside her chest, as if her lungs were being slowly pushed apart and an anvil pressed down on her heart.

Breathing shallowly, she staggered towards the chair, and from there she could grasp one of the banister railings. Three steps up. Hold on tight. Stop, get your breath. Three steps more. Eventually she sprawled upon the bed, reached for the phone and dialled 111. An advisor took details of her symptoms, age, and status (it might almost have been an internet dating site) then 10 minutes of Vivaldi's 'Four Seasons' were followed by a medical professional asking more or less the same questions, then there came the offer of a visit from the paramedics. Ella was too breathless to argue, said it was a waste of NHS time, was relieved to lose the argument.

Drifting on waves of clammy nausea, her vision came and went. The ceiling rotated. After... how long? The rap on her front door was violent, suggesting that it would be broken down if left unopened, and Ella stumbled off the bed, grabbed at a door frame, and fell forward, catching the banister railing just before gravity took over. She got to the door, opened it and found a little girl in a green jacket with a backpack, standing in her doorway.

'Hello there, awright? Are you Ella?' said the child. Ella thought that if she were assigning singing parts in a choir, this little blond girl was first soprano, no question. She stepped back to let her in, fell onto the sofa, and saw that the girl was followed by what appeared to be a tall, loping teenage boy, also wearing a green jacket.

'Lemme jus' hold your hand a minute,' the girl offered, pulling a rubber clothes peg on a wire from a pocket in her pack. She stuck it on Ella's middle finger, and Ella took a deep, painful breath, staring up at the boy whose head seemed to brush the ceiling. She felt the oddity of appearing in her pajamas in front of these children. 'I'm just gonna stick some little stickies on you,' said the girl.

The boy asked politely if he might sit down, did so, and perching on the edge of a recliner, began softly asking questions of the girl, which she answered in numbers something was two hundred over something, and Ella felt a finger being pricked at one point. A number was spoken *soto voce* to the boy who continued to fill in his forms. The girl had produced a thing that looked like a television set with rubber bellows on its sides, and as she read out numbers, the television set reeled off strips of curly paper partially covered in wiggling lines. Ella was asked at one point to stand up, head swimming slightly, and the golden child murmured something about postural hypo... something. 'But only a little bit.'

Ella sat back down without falling. The girl sat on the floor and scrutinised the thin strips of paper, as though examining a till roll in a supermarket. On the top of her head was a soft yellow bun of hair which glistened in the lamplight.

The boy said, 'Sorry, Janey, I'm letting you do all the work.'

'Aw no, you're awright,' said Janey. The vowel stretched itself out and flattened in a way that Ella, feeling a bit better now, recognised as Lancashire speech. A picture rose before her unclouded eyes. She imagined dry stone walls curving across the moors, here and there were short-tailed sheep grazing. A few trees, bent by the wind, sheltered a muddy lane which wound perhaps two hundred yards across the stony ground to a farmhouse. A door opened, and out came the little girl who lived down the lane, a blond ponytail swinging, books in a bag, off to college to do nurse-training.

'I bet you see some interesting things in your job,' Ella said, catching her eye.

'Oh yeah! Last night I delivered my first baby in somebody's house. I came through the door just as the head was surfacing!'

Ella knew she was going to write about all this in her journal. She'd name it, would call it 'The Little Girl who lived Down the Lane.' At any other time it would be impossible to consider such a title without going dark and thinking about murder and child molestation, all the things you can't think about at Christmas. All those other things you can't think about at all if you can help it... Brexit... Donald Trump... stabbings on trains. But now she saw it differently, more hopeful.

Janey was teasing the boy, Matt, about his wife having her first baby this coming March, and how he was going to forget all his medical training and be a scaredy-cat dad on the day. Ella apologised to the young people for calling them out, but Oh No, they said. It wasn't time wasted. They could see things looking a little better on the print-outs. Would she come with them to the hospital, just in case?

No thanks, I'll be fine, Ella told them, smiling. Matt wrote on the form, 'Declines hospital assessment. Has capacity.'

Yes she does, thought Ella. She thought about writing it down in her journal. How could she do Janey justice?

# KEEPING THE PACE

Scalpel slivers living flesh
Erupting reddening petal flames
Making room for...
Tick tick tick.

Easing an inner leaping salmon
Wriggling in a carmine current
Trapped and struggling,
'Til sparking sliders penetrate.

Blindly making their way to
Atrium and ventricle,
A rhythmic steadying
Calming, lightening.

Where before, gagged and throbbing
Trapped petals clotted at
A darkening door....
There is peaceful flowing.

# WITHERED OLIVE BRANCH

Fate awards us
Contemptuous damages when
we make atoms of Saloniki like Guernica,
now Aleppo

A surgeon is beguiled then lost
as he perceives Judith
and pieces of her children
turgid in clotted wine

It is a pyrrhic age and time
when bounty lies in untruth
and echoes of Palmyra sing
where columns stood

Cinnamon and almond once
perfumed this land of dust.

# AN UNSUPPORTED WOMAN

Queuing for the Tuesday weigh-in, Ella slid a hand over her spare tyre. The soft layer offered an inch to be pinched. Signing in she muttered, 'Going to be up today.' Ahead of her in the line was Sandrine, an odd little person, eldest in the class, skeletally thin. Sandrine tottered onto the scale and had her card marked: 'Below goal weight.' Ella knew this because, even at a discreet distance, she could hear their leader Jenny say so. Sandrine stepped sideways off the scale and Jenny set the scale at zero.

Ella sighed and stepped on. 'A pound up this week,' Jenny sympathised. 'You'll soon have that off.' Behind her, the queue stretched the length of the village hall.

All the weighed in members sat in rows making giggling disclosures about who was 'up' in pounds this week and who was 'down', about pieces of cake or cocktails consumed or resisted. Ella found herself sitting next to Sandrine at the end of a row. She stared vacantly ahead, waiting for the queue by the door to dwindle. The scale would go back in its box, applause for those who were 'down' would come next, the Slimmer of the Week would get a Certificate, and forty minutes of aerobics would follow.

Leaping about behind Sandrine at previous classes, Ella had wondered what drove the old lady to attend. Someone whispered that she was 87 and you could believe it, seeing the frail hands waving about, covered in liver spots, and the knees, knarled and slightly bent, unable to straighten during the stretches. The chest was concave, the abdomen slightly convex.

'I say, do you have family nearby?'

Ella realised Sandrine had spoken, wondered who in the modern world still says *'I say—'*. Politeness required a response, a 'not very near, and what about you?' would suffice. But for some reason she answered more literally. 'No, 'she said, 'not at all, and my son and granddaughter are both working in Kenya as it happens.'

'Oh, I loved *Keen-ya*,' Sandrine breathed.

'Don't they say Kenya nowadays?' Ella asked vaguely, looking over her shoulder at the lengthening line.

'People said *Keenya* when I lived there.'

Ella was suddenly curious. Sandrine demurred,' I wouldn't want to bore you.'

For once the post weigh-in chat had become interesting. Ella plied Sandrine with questions and a story emerged, of 11 year-old Sandrine whose father had died on their small farm in the Rift Valley. Mother and daughter were alone on a hundred acres of bush with their servants and field hands. She looked into Sandrine's face and saw nostalgia and fear rekindled in the clouded eyes. She was told about European neighbours stabbed in the night, farmhouses in flames. 'We have to stay on our feet,' Mother kept saying to me, 'because we have nowhere else to go' we could only believe that if our servants were loyal, they were more afraid of other Kikuyu than of us.' Sandrine went on, 'Mother learned that three scars on the back meant they had taken the oath to the Mau Mau that they would kill a European. She asked all our workers to come into the kitchen and she said, "We have been good to you and paid you fairly. Now I want you to take your shirts off," and every one of them had the three scars. My mother said all right, 'Now I want you to take an oath to me. If you have to kill a European it will not be me or my daughter,' and they did.'

Sandrine took a deep breath. 'We stayed on the farm for another seven years, until a relative from England sent us some money and we could get away. All our friends were gone. We left everything behind and took a ship from Mombasa. I saw England for the first time when I was 18.'

'Right, ladies!' Jenny leapt onto the stage, 'Our Slimmer of the Week is'

Ella whispered, 'how did you get through the days, knowing the danger?'

'Mother had to trust our Kikuyu were loyal to us *as well...*' Sandrine folded her chair and pushed it against the wall. Snoop Dog's voice boomed from the speakers. The ladies danced. Sandrine wavered, but she stayed on her feet.

# A FIGURE OF FUN

I used to love going to parties like this. When we were young my sister and I wore out dozens of pairs of dancing shoes. Mama used to beg Papa frequently for a new pair of satin pumps or a dress for each of us when we could no longer find ways of changing them round with fringes and bows. We could not bear to be seen wearing the same things again and again. Even in those early days, Mama never took quite so much notice of me, comparing the two of us and preferring my sister.

Now I peer through the candlelight hardly able to make out the new fashions or even to fix my eye on one or another of my daughters. It is most important to note whether they seem to be dancing with the same partner more than just once or twice. These days candles are dimmer than they used to be. That is it. They must be failing in brilliance and made from cheap tallow.

*Drat the girls!* Why don't they come to me between the dances sometimes? They just trip away into the crowd and are lost, so there is no one to talk to but Mrs. L who is a spiteful creature. She always reminds me that her husband has lately been knighted, I am henceforth to address her as 'my lady'. When I try to converse with her it is hopeless. I can barely hear her remarks above the flutes and strings.

Lady L boasts about her daughter that is the sense of it she talks of the number of young gentlemen who flock about the girl (where? I cannot make them out). I want to tell her that my daughter is dancing, I think, with the elder son of our host or perhaps he *is* our host and I hear myself speaking too loudly. She draws away as if I were shouting, which a gentleman's wife would never do. She looks at me witheringly as do several others. They think me a silly woman, as my husband often reminds me.

My eyes focus for a moment and I see my youngest daughter dancing with an officer. At least I believe it to be she, and I know him to be an officer as he is wearing a red coat. He says something to her as they make a pirouette and as she swings away she laughs out loud across the line of dancers. She is not ladylike but I do love her.

My youngest daughter reminds me of myself when I was a girl. In those days the young gentlemen enjoyed my musical laughter and my brilliance at parties. I knew every step of all the dances – our dancing master Mr. Winthrop (oh, why can I recall his name so easily yet yesterday I forgot to give Cook our order for dinner?)

*Mr. Winthrop only needs to show me once, even the most trying steps, and I know them at once.*

My husband admitted to me after our wedding that he had been shy of dancing with me because I seemed always to be the best in the room. In those days he thought me clever. But he soon learned when he tried to instruct me about the books in his library, that my wit lay only in repartee and dance steps and not, he said, in my brain. My sister's steady good sense was well rewarded. She married first, and her husband was a gentleman whose temperament matched hers. I loved being a bridesmaid then, but felt unmoored when she departed for London with him. Loneliness made me nervous and perhaps a touch more frivolous.

*I am six years of age and she must be eight. Mama is boxing my ears and telling me to hush, to stop being so silly. Tears drop from my cheeks and my hot, red chin -- but I cannot stop myself. 'Where is my sister gone? Eleanor, Eleanor where are you?*

It was even worse when we grew up and she married. Now I can't remember where she had gone on that earlier day. I only recall how lost I was without her.

Mama never took much notice of me, preferring my sister and comparing us to one another.

I look round the room and can make out nothing but a sea of blurred colour. I can barely perceive the dancers and were it not for the music, I could not tell a longways set from a round. My husband and my children find me difficult I know, but who would be easy in their mind given my peculiar circumstances?

My mind drifts because I cannot see well, and the thought that makes me silly and anxious is of having nowhere to live in the future. My husband has left off conversing with me and hides away with his books. He simply will not see that when he dies, if my daughters have not married well we might all go to the almshouse. He shuts me out and makes fun of me because he believes the trouble to be all my own fault. I gather that it is, but why?

I never chose the pain of childbed only to produce five daughters. Time after time, even before thinking to rise from each blood-soaked couch my first question to the servant would be, 'What is it? Boy or girl?' She would smile at me, but did I see malice in her eye? It seemed she witnessed my fear and saw my disappointment. 'You have a fine baby girl – a pretty baby girl – a perfect – a lively – a healthy –.' And so it would go, year after year, until at last I screamed, 'Take it away! I never want to hear it squall or see its nasty purple face!'

Very odd it is that the last one, whom I could hardly bear to nurse, has become my favourite.

My husband has a favourite, next to the eldest, and I have mine. Very different girls they all are, one from another, but I love the youngest best.

He has told me many times: Our doctor says if a woman fails to produce sons to inherit, then it is entirely her fault. It is there in her head and womb, that failure. I must believe it to be true even though I prayed as often as any mother alive that I might produce a son. The house and everything we have is entailed to my husband's cousin. I knew it, and yet I could give life only to girls.

He hates me, I think. That is why he ignores the danger. He belittles me laughingly to all the family, and even does it, outrageously, in front of the servants. My daughters ignore every word I say except the one true thing, that they must get husbands. Perchance they would find it easier if I were calm and unaffected, a credit to them all. If I could simply not be, as they say, a silly woman.

They tell me I speak too loudly, but I can barely hear them as they say it.

I must stop thinking about this, it is driving me mad. A gentleman stands nearby, watching the dancers. He is speaking to his friend, almost near enough for me to hear him perhaps he *means* me to hear him. His gaze seems to rest on me for a moment before he turns toward one of the young ladies. Is it my daughter? I think I hear him say he is not 'tempted' by any woman in the room. What is his name, nasty man? It could be my next to eldest daughter Lizzie he is looking at. It is probably her as she is the only one wearing that shade of palest pink. He is a friend of our host. Could his name be Dancy? My brain whirls. The name begins with D.... Could it be Darcy?

# LEAVING THE SUBSTRATE

---

**Metamorphosis,** *noun.* Meaning: transformation, mutation, transfiguration, conversion, remodeling, restyling, reconstruction, reordering

**Digital,** *adjective*: Meaning: (1) to represent data as numbers, or (2) to express a varying physical quantity such as sound or light waves by means of discrete signals usually numbers in the binary system
Encarta Dictionary.

'You got in all right, good. So darling, here he is. Do you believe me now?'

Danielle was a little uncomfortable at being called darling. She peered at the object. 'This is Harvey?'

'Um-hm. Just as I told you. It's D.H. – Digital Harvey. Kind of amusing, isn't it?'

'What's amusing? Oh, your surname's Lawrence so he's D. H. Lawrence. Yeah, that's kinda cute.'

'He always liked his nooky, Harvey did – *loved* it in fact before he was diagnosed, so we both got a kick out of the D.H. Lawrence idea.'

And the retro casing? Was that his idea or yours?'

'Mine, actually. We were talking it over before he... transmogrified...' Billie-Ann grinned at her new consultant, 'and we thought it would be fun to present the futuristic Harvey in an old-fashioned console that looks like a twentieth century radiogram d'you remember them? No, you're too young, of course you wouldn't.'

'Did you say, "*We* thought?" Danielle reflected, eyeing her new client.

'Well yes, it's easier to say 'we thought' now, since he was uploaded into the Cloud. I draw down most of him here.' Billie-Ann touched her forehead. He does all his creative stuff through me and he gets his sensory input through the console in the corner. I just have to switch on the chip here,' she tapped a raised area between her eyebrows, 'and now he gets everything – sounds, smells. We even devised a digitised version of taste and touch, although that works less well.'

Billie-Ann gave a coy smile. 'He gets a little tingle of pleasure when I use this.' She opened a drawer in Harvey's casing and drew out a pink box bearing the logo: Ann Summers Upbeat Ultra. A light on the console began to pulsate rapidly. 'Not now, Harvey! Danielle's here. No, you cheeky thing. Stop it! '*No' means 'No', remember?* Billie-Ann paused. She said, 'I added a bit to the uploading just a few feminist concepts that could be represented as binary numbers, to make him a bit less... dominant.'

There was a grunt from the cabinet.

'So let's get this straight,' Danielle said. 'I just need to be sure what you want, so we'll recap. When Harvey's body reached the end stage and all his organs were shutting down, the two of you opted for Whole Brain Emulation. Both of you got his consciousness loaded onto a chip and in it went,' Danielle pointed at the space between her client's eyebrows. 'And now that the Catastrophe is here and the collapse of civilisation is inevitable you want me and one or two of my carefully selected colleagues, who will also be signing Non-Disclosure Agreements, to find a way out for you two, a way off the planet. You get to escape. Forget everybody else.'

'Bloody hell, yes!' David Tennant blurted from a speaker in the console.

Danielle jumped. 'That sounds like an actor who used to play Dr. Who back in the twenty-teens!'

'Yes, I know,' Billie-Ann concurred. 'We stripped out David Tennant's voice from a twentieth century TV recorder we found in the boot of in an old petrol car we'd hidden and kept as an antique. And because Harvey was going to be D.H. Lawrence, I experimented with Nottinghamshire accents at first. But none of them had anything like the necessary vocabulary. Go on Harvey, say 'life extension concepts are themselves accelerating'.'

'Life extension concepts are themselves accelerating!' proclaimed the Tenth Doctor.

'Thank you, Harvey,' said his wife.

'And I've got a few more things to say—' The Doctor ejaculated.

'Wait a minute!' Danielle interrupted. 'Just hang on here. You both know, don't you, that Non-Disclosure Agreements are worthless there'll be no Courts to enforce them, and no fines and no prisons and no anything. The end is NOW, pretty much.

'Once the North Koreans did the Chinese a favour and accidentally blew up most of Hong Kong,' Danielle's voice rose, 'and the best of Silicon Valley got burnt by sheet lightening when the rainforests were stripped out and the Amazon warehouses were looted, now a million refugees infected with mutating viruses are making their way across the interior.' Danielle almost whispered, 'There is no point to any of this. It's over.

'And,' she continued, 'you might at least have considered other humans, the ones with no escape. You were worried I'd have a problem getting past your security guards at the bottom of the hill? *Ha, ha.* Most of them have already dismantled the electronic pain collars you made them put on in exchange for self-generating protein food and bomb-proof shelters. It was easy to bribe the others. You two are already'

'Already *what*?' Billie-Ann and Harvey shouted in unison. 'Defenceless? The last person who said that,' Billie-Ann rattled on, teeth chattering, 'was a scientist called Douglas Rushcough or some other unhealthy-sounding name, and the one before him had a Chinese name. They're both locked up in the junk-house where we keep the petrol cars left over from the fossil fuel days—if those guys are still viable.'

'You'll never get out of here on your own,' said Danielle, with prescience.

The mole-like centre between Billie-Ann's eye-brows pulsated and she pressed a button on her left thigh, summoning the security guards.

Nobody came. Danielle walked out. She didn't even need to run. Had there been any calendars kicking around, the extinction of Billie-Ann and Harvey would have taken place on a Tuesday.

# SWINESONG

---○---

**Prologue.**

Today is the last day. Tomorrow, Trevor's General Licence will be invalid and that's a damn shame. Small farmers have little enough to defend against crows that peck out the eyes of lambs and piglets. He hates crows, and fires at will when he spots one.

Today he is in a filthy mood, filthy is the word. Late yesterday evening as the sun was setting, he had found a phone partially covered in dry leaves. He had switched it on hoping to find details of its owner. Nothing. He clicked on Gallery, and up came what appeared to be a selfie. The picture showed the head and shoulders of a leather-jacketed individual, a man. Rough looking. Trevor opened several more images, landscape, buildings, a house – his house. And then.

Then he came upon a photo of his seven year-old daughter, Arabella. And another. One was a rear view:

she was holding a bucket, leaning down, picking up windfall apples from the ground, under a tree outside their kitchen door. There were more. In all he counted twenty-one. Twenty-one pictures of his daughter, leaning forward so that her sundress fell away from her little shoulders, reaching up to pick a flower from a shrub. He grinds his teeth. The man in the jacket had been in his garden, taking pictures of his child.

Today moving quietly in his woodland, armed, he sees the man in the leather jacket. This is the image on the phone.

Petunia is a fine Tamworth and she likes the forest. She relishes the mossy undergrowth, draws in the smells of wormy earth and nibbles on insects. Mushrooms are another pleasure, and if she has good luck, the small explosions of bitter brown dust tell her of puffballs in the dappled clearings. Today there is a new smell. It reminds her of dead mice but is much richer and sweeter. It makes her think of the farm. She does not know why. Then she remembers the smell of the little two-leg girl who now and then brings apples and carrots to the fence and passes them to her.

The breeze draws her further into the bushy areas, and she has to push through creepers and low branches to find the source of the alluring odour. Nesting birds sound warning calls. Eventually she comes upon a shape half hidden under a bush and covered by a beardy rambler. The smell is all around her now and in its centre lies a two-leg creature, one she does not know. It lies quite still. She is afraid. She is curious.

Petunia circles round the bush, peering through the creeper. The creature does not move. She taps at it with her front foot and jumps back in case it comes to life. It is still. One of its long arms extends so that it is within her reach, its chubby front paw open under her nose. She snuffles at it and bites through the soft part, nipping at the bony bit inside. The bone snaps and she draws the piece into her mouth, tasting the fresh blood and meat. It's good. She eats up its whole paw.

It's hard to get any further up the creature's front paw because the leg and the whole upper body are encased in a cover that smells of cow hide. She tears at the hide but it won't surrender its contents so she snuffles under the body and finds the other front paw. It is good, so she eats that. Its big round head comes next. She cracks its jaw and delights in its thick tongue. She works hard at the eye brows, breaking the brittle bones and making her way upwards along the skull. Oh, delicious! Once she gets into that, there is a wrinkled grey mass very silky and oozing more blood. Petunia eats as much as she can hold. She even swallows a nasty metallic thing that's stuck in the wrinkles. When she is full she wanders off to the edge of the forest and has a nap in the sun.

The next morning Petunia returns to that special place in the forest where she had found the two-leg, but already her nose tells her something is wrong. Now she isn't the only one who's interested. Her special meal is covered in a feathery brownish tent, a shroud that moves and flutters. It pushes parts of itself out of the way so that other parts of it can get a better mouthful. Some of the quilled ones lift their heads and flap at her and some of them leave the carcass to dive at Petunia, biting her with their curved beaks. She draws back sharply and turns away. She had seen the feathered ones before. Once, they came when there was a dead calf; she knows it is no good.

They are too many.

The next day is no good at all. Petunia has a look, but there is strange striped tape all around the bushes and lots of two-legs dressed in white suits and booties are walking around her dead creature. She truffles away and gets a bit of fungus to chew. Then she trots back across the fields, manuring them as she goes.

As she approaches the fence, she sees the little two-leg girl waiting for her with bucket of spotty carrots. 'Good morning Petunia, my favourite piggy, here you are. I've got something for you. Look at these!' The little girl pushes at the bucket but she can't get it all the way through the gap in the fence. She extends a hand through another small gap and tips the upper rim so the bucket will shuffle out its contents, dropping them onto the ground in front of her friend. Petunia is delighted and salivating; she sniffs at the little hand.

'Arabella! Lunch is ready. Leave that filthy old pig alone. They bite, you know. Come in and wash your hands!'

At briefing, the Chief Inspector growls to his team that they'll need to wait for tests to be done. On this corpse, there's no ID, no face, no prints, and crucially no sign of a murder weapon.

Arabella has had a very gentle explanation. She is sad but she knows Petunia is going away this afternoon in a lorry to a place that she calls the Abba Twa.

A small piece of lead lies in a well-manured field somewhere. Ready for the plough.

# SAL

When you live in a trailer park and your car's been repossessed, you don't get much of a choice about what you have for breakfast. I'm walking to the Texaco station and they don't take Food Stamps, so I'm just going to get me a family pack of Doritos.

I'd like to have somebody to walk up here with, some girlfriend to talk to now that it looks like Doug isn't coming back. All I got left of him to prove he was even there is an eagle's head key ring he gave me. I've got it in my pocket now, and I've got my sweaty hand in there holdin' it, turning it over and feeling it kick against the ham of my hand. It makes me think about the baby I almost had with Doug but it came away and there was nobody to tell about it so I buried it under the trailer. Now I'm just walking up the road under a bleached sky.

My favourite boots are headed for the scrap heap, just like me I guess. They were so pretty when Doug said he'd buy them for me. He lost a lot of money that weekend at the Troubadour Casino so in the end I spent my last week's pay on them. At least I had something to show for my money. I'd seen these boots in the C & W Store. They had tooled leather slashes up the sides and squared off toes and high heels that curved forwards so they'd stay in the stirrups as if I was riding in a rodeo. Ha, ha.

I'm still wearing the boots to remember him by but they aren't so good for walking in. My feet are moving around inside them where I'm sweating so much. Bare feet inside cowboy boots, Lord have mercy. They look pretty good with cut off shorts – they just don't feel so good. And the heels are going over at the sides. If I step sideways on a rock I'm gonna break my goddam ankle.

Last summer was the only time Doug and I ever went on a trip. He said for once in his life he wanted to gamble in style so we went to Nero's in Vegas. I was scared to death of the place. Las Vegas is like Sodom and Gomorrah in the Bible. We had to pass through all these towers and showers of lights everywhere and crowds and horns blowing and fights here and there.

Once we got to Nero's and passed through the ground floor where all the slot machines were bleating at each other and ever'body was staring at them with their dead swivel eyes trying to conjure money out of the metal boxes, we got to the desk where we could pick up our keys.

We got in the elevator and went on up to the room and I dumped everything out of my suitcase onto the bed but Doug didn't even do that. He had a pee and then went straight on down to the floor where they played poker and blackjack.

Our bathroom had a bath with gold taps and water jets which I had never seen before except on TV on "Lives of the Rich and Famous" so I filled up the tub and got in. I wonder how many girls did what I did. If you've never spread your legs in front of one of those jets well... you don't need to know about it.

I knew Doug wouldn't be back for hours, so I went down in the basement to where those Mexican girls do the massages. They just caress you and then punch you a bit, just to let you know who's boss in case you say anything ugly to them.

I could smell the sweet flower oils mixed with chlorine from the swimming pool. In the pool there was this guy with his girl just necking and making out with each other and twining their feet under the water.

On the other side of the pool was a chrome ladder that led up to an archway hung with golden horse shoes and nylon gladiolas and roses. I'm remembering it clear as anything. I'm watching that guy and the girl as they climb up the ladder and stand under the arch dripping in their bathing suits. Then, God have mercy, a man dressed up like a preacher comes out from underneath the arch and says, 'We are gathered here....' They're gettin' married straight out of the pool!

At the time I was so taken by it I forgot to give the massage girl a tip so she came out and gave me a dirty look. I gave her a dollar and then she went to be a witness at the wedding.

I'm thinking back and it's like I'm there again. It's Sunday, and I'm considering... if Doug has a win he'll be in a good mood. Tomorrow morning we can have a champagne breakfast to top him up and then we'll head for the pool.

It almost works! I get him all the way down there and then he sees the arch. It sobers him up real quick. He's lookin' like a stag that raises its head all of a sudden when it hears a gun being cocked. He stands up in the pool lookin' at the arch and I think he knows what I've got him into. I can see the cogwheels going around in his brain. Nevada is the only state where you can get married in a rush like going to the supermarket or putting gas in your car. It's now or never, yes or no.

He looks around at me like a deer would look it was trapped. Then he stares back up at the arch.

I watch as his whole body relaxes. His fists unclench and he lays back in the green chemical water and floats on his back. He's singing a bit of a country song

I look closely at the arch. Propped up at its foot among the plastic flowers is a little sign: Closed on Mondays.

That was the nearest we ever got, and really it was me that got us there. Doug had a loss at the tables that night, a big one. He was grumpy all the way home.

*Al and me have been married 18 years today. We live on a little biddy farm on Route 501. Every Sunday morning he says to me, 'Alma, you ready to go to Church?' and we get in the truck and go up the road to the First Baptist. I love that Church. I've been going there since years before I was big enough to think about marrying Al. He and I met at primary school and then at the 4H Clubs. We went to their dances and it was just natural. We got married when I was 17. By the time I was 20 we were good and ready to start a family but nothing happened. Every Sunday we'd both go to church and we prayed for a child, but nothing. Then down the road on the small holding some people moved in and there was this little girl, Sal. She had five brothers and she was the only girl. I think they gave her a bit of a rough time one way and another. She was so little and knock-kneed. She used to come to the fence and stare at my flowers.*

*I started talking to her, and then I let her come inside my front yard and help me with the weeding. She was such a sweet thing. I used to think of Sal as my little* girl. Her family didn't seem to take much note of her, and they never bothered to go to Church.

One day I asked Sal's mother if we could take her to Church with us and she jus' said, 'I reckon.' She had what looked like a black eye and she was all worn out, you could tell.

Then it got so that Sal was more at our house than at her own. It was fine. She was happy to be with us and going to the Sunday school at First Baptist and Bible School in the summers.

That is, it was fine until Doug turned up out of no-where. I said to her, 'Darlin', don't get your head turned by the first one that comes along.'

This Douglas was a lot older than Sal, my Sal as I used to call her.

Before he came I recall saying to her, 'Darlin', would you like to join the Baptist Girls Fellowship? They have a beautiful ceremony where you get your Virgin Ring that you keep on your finger 'til you get married, and she said yes she would.

It's as if it was yesterday. Al and I take Sal to watch the total immersion in the shallow pool where two streams meet. Our Pastor brings out the last young man all soaking wet from the pool and blesses him. It's Lester from the big farm up the road and the Pastor tells him this is the dividing line between lost and found and you are going to walk with Jesus for all of your life. I keep imagining Sal marrying Lester and wearing a white *dress. In my dream Lester takes the virgin ring from her finger and replaces it with a gold band and I can barely sing the hymn through my tears.*

*Bang! Here comes Doug and it's all gone. She hardly ever comes to our house, anymore, sneaking off with Doug all the time. Doug says he's a veteran, but I don't know a veteran of what exactly. Even though I see that look of cunning in his eyes I think maybe it'll all be all right. We'll get him to come to Church and he'll find Jesus. Then they sneak off for good.*

*He took my little girl away with him.*

*She left me the sweetest little note, but she still went. Maybe she always had a little bit of the Devil in her. I don't know if she ever told me the whole truth about anything.*

*I've prayed and prayed about it, but I can't make it out. Al says to just let it go. She's not ours. I go to see her mother at the small-holding but she just shrugs. That made me sadder than anything. I think Sal is 15, but I'm not even sure about that.*

Things aren't so bad now. I was so down on my luck I'd have shot myself. Or maybe not. Anyway, Charlie and Henrietta who own the trailer park knew Doug had left me and I didn't have any money and no way to get a job because how would I get there?

They asked me if I'd like to go to Church with them. It was funny how quick I said yes. I couldn't think what to wear. I cut the top off my old black dress and tucked it into my green skirt like it was a blouse and left those terrible old boots in the trailer. I'd got a pair of sandals that weren't too bad and I tied my hair back. For some reason I took Doug's silver eagle key ring off the trailer key and left it in a drawer.

Their Church reminded me of the one I used to go to years ago with Al and Alma.

That was a long, long time ago. I more or less run the trailer park now, for Charlie and Henrietta. They're getting to be too old to do much, but we're getting by.

# TWENTY-TWENTY VISIONS

A bruise can be beautiful if you look at it closely. 'Objectively' might be a better word. A sea of purple spreads beneath the outer layer of me, edged in sunset gold.

On the other hand, if you look at someone's arm, someone white that is, and you see a bruise, it looks like damage. The colour is lurid against white skin, the contrasting shades harsh. If someone sees it they are alarmed and will ask what happened to you, even if the answer is 'nothing very much.'

The bruise that must have been left as Officer Derek Chauvin lifted his knee off George Floyd's neck might hardly have been visible, being black on black, to anyone but a member of Floyd's family or a forensic investigator. But it was *very much indeed*. All the tissues under his skin must have burst. Blood would have pooled in his windpipe. It caused crowds to face riot shields, churches to ring with singing, words to be written and chanted. Banners were unfurled, millions marched, statues tumbled, crowds risked infection, touched each other, and faced their opponents – human and microbial.

Hello journal. Tonight I started with a preface because the tangle of substance and trivia in the life going on around me looks impenetrable, hopeful, fraught. It's everybody's lives, god knows, not just mine.

Living on your own makes you consider solitude. It can be a freeing thing to be savoured, and a torture you can almost taste. It's unhealthy to be too much alone. Scientists even say it makes you sick, and we have to be guided by the science. Now, after ten weeks of slothful aloneness we are all invited to mingle, bewildered, at a prescribed distance from each other. As we stumble out of lockdown, we find ourselves cooked in the stifling heat of early summer. In some cases it bubbles up to murder. In others it prompts small garden parties.

The phone beeps. 'Next Tuesday come and sit in our garden in the sunshine,' says Godfrey's text.

I answer, 'That would be lovely.' Is it? He and Ida haven't been out of their house in nearly three months. He's been a 'shielded person' who wouldn't let Ida out of his sight in case something stuck to her and she brought home germs to him. Volunteers have left bags outside their door. But solitude, and time spent together for the two of them must almost be solitude, has prompted him to ask me to come and visit, and the word 'lovely' to be my answer. It's agreed. I am probably one of a series of individuals as the lockdown eases, brought to their garden to amuse Ida.

'By the way,' my phone screen message says, 'to avoid embarrassment, please don't ask to use our toilet.'

I consider. It's twenty miles to Upper Dorford by the canal, forty kilometers of country road where tractors dawdle and cyclists drift across the tarmac to avoid bees. Forty minutes each way, an hour or two on their flower-bordered lawn. Three hours minimum. Hmm. My unmanicured fingers tap out a reply: 'Let me suggest something. In case of need, we could resort to hospital protocol hand sanitiser, throw away paper towels for door knobs, all that stuff. Wash hands, sing "Happy Birthday" twice.'

My phone beeps back. Brushing the fringe out of my eyes I read Godfrey's response, at least I presume it's Godfrey's. Of the two of them, he's the greatest hypochondriac: 'The initial decision still stands,' the screen says, 'Perhaps you feel you can't hold out, or our other friends are younger, live nearer, or have stronger bladders.'

I am sitting quite still, looking down at slightly swollen ankles. Which of them wrote that message? Does it matter? Some sensation, a cousin of road rage, lifts my blood pressure, tightens my upper lip. The impulse to refuse their invitation is almost uncontrollable. Why should I convey my germy body up the road, pass it through their garden gate, and lower it onto a searing hot wrought iron chair in their garden? 'Piss off.' My finger hovers over the letter 'P' on the keypad. It hesitates.

Godfrey is a founder member of Gleeful, our choir, one block in my fortress against the ravages of aloneness. All my clubs and classes and worthy causes, fitness groups and eco-friendly gatherings of right-minded people which I've drifted towards and settled into are on the brink of extinction. We could all die of social distancing. We could all die. I'd be found only because a certain smell would perfume the near end of my street. And now, as I contemplate my own extinction, comes an invitation to Godfrey and Ida's summer garden.

Can I afford to let fly at him? What if some of these human gatherings should start to reassemble without me because I've taken the huff? Better to grind my dentures for a day or two, take the stew off the heat. They can only entertain people one at a time, and only in the garden. He probably realises that in shielding his lady wife, he has driven her crazy.

Today is Wednesday. Thursday goes by. And Friday. It occurs to me that my bladder, strong or weak, is not the problem here. The problem is Godfrey and Ida's *house*. The whole place is an arty death-trap. A single banister leads up their creaking staircase as you climb to the smallest room. Germs cling to that sticky railing; whatever mutating bugs they've got could stick to my hand, covered though the hand may be in green sanitiser. At last I know what to say to Ida and Godfrey. 'I think you're right,' I tap, 'your house isn't designed for guests to visit your lavatory safely. So maybe another time, when it's all over and we can see what the new normal looks like.'

'Oh no, you must come,' he taps. Ida and I have decided you can use the toilet on our boat.'

I think, *Yuk*. But… isolation is driving me out like a combustion engine.

'One Hundred Years of Solitude' writes Gabriel Garcia Marquez; 'Slaves of Solitude' says Patrick Hamilton. What do they know about it? Marquez's book is about households full of funny people burning their hands in the woodstove and flying up to heaven while pegging out the washing, and Hamilton's novel talks about a dozen or so survivors all cramped in a boarding house after the Blitz. None of them knows a sodding thing about actually living on your own day after day, month after month until you drop off your perch. God, I love self-pity. It's almost as good as the thoughtful empathy of other people. I'm owed some respite from all this. I've earned it. I deserve some company.

Chug, chug, up the road, along the lanes…. Inside a cool box I've got individually wrapped chocolates for them in a sealed plastic bag.

Ida and Godfrey are an elderly couple, almost as old as me. Time takes its toll differently on all of us, and the infirmities of others are a subject of fascination to us as we age. Godfrey's front teeth are slightly crossed, and appear to lengthen as the years pass. They lend sibilance to the purity of his baritone solos. Amusingly, his toes cross over each other in exactly the same way. You can note this on the days he chooses to wear sandals and his hairy crisscross toes are on display. His spine is curved in a rounded arch, like half of a navel orange, making the size of his tummy unguessable. Ida's back is straight enough, but her nose curves upwards and I picture it buried in the fleshly folds of Godfrey's front as she forages for his member, hoping to revive it after years of a long marriage. One's own organic deterioration is placed cheerfully to one side during these musings.

They've told me to let myself in at the garden gate. I twist the handle and it doesn't budge. I push the gate. I shout. No answer. Retreating, I stumble back over the rough turf towards the car, almost relieved. But just as I reach the pavement I hear Godfrey's accusing voice,

'You didn't push the gate hard enough.' He's holding it open. I was taking the coward's way out, but now there's no escape.

Facial muscles assembled in a smile, I greet them. 'Didn't like to come empty-handed, so I brought you some chocolates'

Godfrey approves. 'That's fine. Leave them in their bag and put them inside the back door of the conservatory. After 24 hours we can have them.'

I am directed to a wrought iron chair, a little ouchy-hot but bearable through my capris. Ida and Godfrey seat themselves on a wooden bench ten feet away from me, and I am now six years old. Mummy and Daddy are sitting on the bench side by side, looking at their only child and reproving her for a venal misdemeanor – could it be germy hands?

On a table at my side is a charming antique cup full of strawberries and a plate bearing a loaf cake topped with shiny chocolate sauce. 'We've made a cake in your honour,' says Godfrey. Is this a test? 'Go on,' he says. 'Cut yourself a piece. 'I gag down a bit, picturing them icing the cake, dabbing at stray bits of frosting, licking their fingers, and poking at the cake again. We chat. The earth gradually turns away from the sun on its immense axis and I am in the shadow. Ida is too hot. She wants to be in the shade. I get up cheerfully, offering to swap places and she rises. Godfrey *shrieks*. 'No! You mustn't sit on the bench. It's not distanced enough from me, and Ida mustn't sit in a chair you've sat on. Your hand would have touched the table. She might pick a strawberry from the cup.' Ida says she has a headache. She stumps off into the sanctum of their house.

Godfrey, unfazed by this, says, I've discovered a new footpath near here. Must show you. You'll love it.' I rise again from my sweaty iron chair. 'But first,' he says, 'you must use the loo on the boat! We've primed the stopcocks for you.'

You know the way you can 'listen' to your stomach to decide if you're hungry before you eat something? There's a bladder equivalent, isn't there? As a yoga teacher would put it, you *turn your awareness* to the neck of your bladder deep inside. Do you feel the pressure? Would you feel it if instructed to visit the toilet by a *man*, by somebody else's husband?

Whether I feel pressure or not I'm making my way down 150 feet of garden to the towpath to visit a chemical toilet on a boat, to be polite. The path is three steps down from their garden gate. I totter down the stone stairs and step onto the gangplank. There is a rail just within reach (is it clean?), breathe in, twist the door handle and step down into the cabin, my feet making the deep echo you hear as the hull tips sideways in the water. I find a page of instructions. Pumps here, switches there, under the sink (where?) Oh, under the hinged black glass paneled worktop that conceals the sink. Flip the switch, turn around, slide into the cubicle door, peer into a green chemical pool, try to flush, water won't come. Oh god, oh god.

Exit the boat, return along the garden path, confess I don't understand the instructions, receive a lesson, go back and get on board, misjudge, lose my balance, and scrape my arm nastily to avoid falling in the water. There'll be a bruise just here.

Godfrey's newly discovered footpath turns out to be one for full length s and trainers which I'm not wearing. Grateful to the stinging nettles, I excuse myself and thank him, mumble a wish that Ida's headache gets better, and escape to my car. Gears engaged, the road beckons. A bruise is already rising on my forearm.

Heading home on a single track lane, with a sky the deep blue of late afternoon, I see a muntjac nimbly leap into view and make off again into the undergrowth. What a treat it is to see them on wooded lanes, with their barrel bellies on sturdy little legs. Having got through the garden party I feel now that I've earned these summer blessings: wildflowers, muntjacs, bird song.

Rounding a tight corner in the winding lane, edged as it is with cow parsley and buttercups, I slam hard on the brake. Inches from the bonnet of my little car is a black wall with four chrome rings in its centre. Is this an Audi? It has huge wheels like a 4 by 4, and emits a self-satisfied purr. I know this because my engine has cut out and I'm still holding the brake handle in my sweaty left hand. The thing, this Chelsea Tractor, stands part way across the road, both its doors open, almost touching the edges of the lane. A pale, well-dressed couple are out of the big vehicle and are screaming at something. Just beyond their open driver's side door is a helmeted black man on a bicycle, resting one foot in the wild flowers and one on a pedal.

The couple are shouting that the man has cut across their path and he answers that the right of way was his. Despite their noise, he says that they crossed his path and appeared to use their car as a weapon to knock him off his bike.

'Did you *hear* that?' the woman screeches, 'he said "weapon" you heard him! He's threatening us, he's talking about weapons.'

By this time I'm out of my car. I'm hearing myself interrupt, 'That isn't what he said.' Another car brakes behind mine. A man gets out and joins me, tells them to leave the guy alone. The couple shout back a few times at the cyclist and at us but by now they can see that the odds have altered. As I get out a phone and start to press the video button, they seem to think better of it. They get back in their shiny beast, more like a Minotaur than a car, and there is a slamming of doors. They screech away.

Well how nice that 'we' feels we, me and the new arrival, ask the black guy if he is all right. He says yes, and oddly he then says, 'Those people must not be from around here.' He is forgiving us for being the same col-our as *those* people. In the moment it seems we are the folks from round here, we and he are a threesome, and *they are the others.* How good is that?

I look down at the purpling bruise on my arm, a badge of courage in coping with my little life. I think about George Floyd's neck, and the tangled wider life.

Journal, I wouldn't tell anybody this but you.

# GILDA

To begin with, the gate wouldn't open and that was a bad sign. She believed that if a house wanted you inside, it wouldn't be any trouble to get at it and into it. Houses that welcomed you were the ones that offered an easy entrance. Their doors had well-oiled locks with keys that felt smooth in your hand, made by locksmiths who ground each one with care. Good locks opened with hardly a click, indoors or outdoors, on garages, outbuildings, humble sheds, front doors, back doors, and even gates.

'Mind you,' Gilda said to Archie, 'I don't care for those horrid gates that force you to get out of your car and punch in a code before they'll acknowledge you. No,' she told Archie who had been dead for nine years, 'I don't like snooty gates. They're the sort that have a security box just out of your reach so you have to get out of the car, punch in the numbers, jump back in, then put the car in gear and step on the accelerator before they change their minds and shut the gate in your face. Don't you just hate that kind?

'With this gate, there's none of that nonsense. You're supposed to just get out and slip the latch; give it a push and it swings open. But no. It's stuck and you have to heave like buggery and then it screeches open very slowly, all the way through a ten foot arc.' She performed the operation, extending both arms and putting her back into it. The gate shrieked as if in pain. Grudgingly it gave in.

The house spread out in a dip in the land at the end of a misty drive shrouded in laurels on both sides. Standing in the middle of a couple of acres, its east wing was overhung by the branches of a large sycamore. A pond lay in front of the house as if guarding the door. She parked there and got out, leaving Archie's ashes in a brushed steel coffee mug under the gear stick.

Grinding her shoes on deep gravel, she turned towards the pond. The sun was setting and there was no reflection on the murky water. No ducks greeted her, and no fish stirred. The pond was newtless, frogless, toadless. Weeds surrounded it, and even they were in poor health. Midges skirted the surface.

Turning to the house, Gilda took a Chubb key out of her bag and tried to twist it in the round hole in the door. It resisted. 'See there?' she said to Archie. 'Didn't you know it would be like this?' Eventually the lock yielded with a scratch and a clunk. Unaccountably another one had been fitted, perhaps later. She repeated the process, this time with a Yale key. This one strained her fingers, turned with her effort, and turned again.

She pushed at the door and in a flash a spotted cat shot through the opening, dodged her bag and flew into the laurels. Gilda shoved the door fully open at last, and was hit by the smell of cat litter unchanged for a day or more. There are some smells that assault your nose with certainty. You are in no doubt what they are: death, disinfectant, and cat pee.

She searched the baronial kitchen, checking one cupboard after another until she found an open bag of cat litter. Tipping out the contents of the litter tray into a plastic bag, Gilda told Archie that there were times when you wished you had a third hand to hold your nose when you did jobs like this. She pitched the bag of wet litter out of the kitchen door and refilled the tray.

Her hands needed a wash, and she did this before calling Maureen at her home. 'Sorry to bother you after hours,' Gilda said into the phone, 'but what does your copy of the contract say, about the dates of this job?' She was told that according to the paperwork, the start date was today, but the customer had seemed vague when the booking was made, demented actually. What was the problem?

Gilda told her contact from PetPals, 'It just seems as if they left the house early yesterday, or maybe even the day before. The place is creepy and it stinks. There were no lights left on when I got here, no security on the gate—anybody could've been in here--and that cat, the one I'm supposed to look after, he's bolted. There's no cat flap and the thing's been shut in here for I don't know how long.'

'There's no permissions on this paperwork,' Maureen said comfortably. As if adding insult to injury she said, 'You're not entitled to use any of their food, except food for the cat of course. I hope you've brought your own grub because I looked the place up on Google Earth and there's no shop for miles.'

'There's nothing here to tempt me,' said Gilda, eyeing a bag of Scotch Oats. It bore a use-by date in September of the previous year. 'I've got some crackers and a bit of cheese, and some teabags,' she went on, putting the phone in the crook of her collarbone. She found her way around the house as she talked, pushing open doors with her free hand, turning on each light with relief. 'There's no TV and no note about Wi-Fi codes or a password. Did they tell you anything?'

'Not a blinking thing,' said Maureen after a slight pause. Gilda could hear the theme tune from a well-known soap opera at Maureen's end of the connection. 'Just that it's agreed you're not to leave the place after dark and you're not to be away more than an hour during the day. No deliveries expected, and you're not to have visitors or let anybody in.'

'Except the cat,' Gilda said.

'Except the cat. I have to go,' and Maureen, doubt-less distracted by something on her screen, hung up.

By midnight, there was still no sign of the nameless cat. Gilda had been out once, with a torch and a can of WD40 she had found in a cupboard. She oiled the gate and the front door locks to make it easier to get out if she needed to. Then she called kitty-kitty a couple of times into the tapping leaves of the laurels.

Back in the house, she patrolled the ground floor, checking the doors and the french windows which were brushed by shrubs in the evening wind. Night fell. The house creaked as it cooled. No thermostat awakened the boiler. It was April, but cold as stone and she wrapped herself in her sleeping bag in the front room, sitting on a deep-seated chair that seemed to have been designed for someone with very long legs.

After a time, her back ached, so she moved to an-other chair. Drawing it up towards french windows shrouded in musty damask, she pulled open one curtain and peered out in case the cat was there waiting. This chair was low to the ground, possibly a Victorian nurs-ing chair. In this one, her hips began to play up as she leaned close to the glass, trying to see past her own re-flection.

By one o'clock in the morning, Gilda told Archie that she was giving in. She opened the kitchen door and put out a bowl of water and another of tinned cat food, locked the door, and made her way back to the front room. She sat back down, this time finding an easy chair, the most comfortable of the lot.

She promised Archie she would wait another ten minutes. If there was no sign of that bloody cat she told him, she was going to bed.

She started to nod off. Admitting defeat, Gilda dragged herself up the creaking stairs, bag heavy on her shoulder. She fancied she heard a noise. She could have sworn something, or someone, had vanished from the master bedroom seconds before she opened the door. She saw a marble-topped dressing table and a king-size bedstead. Nothing more. No sheets, no mattress even, just flat worm-eaten slats across the bed frame. She told Archie to remind her she was being silly, but checked the dusty floor under the bed anyway, and opened the wardrobe. A fusty coat or two hung there. No sign of anything or anyone.

The next bedroom door opened almost by itself. She snapped on an overhead bulb and gazed at four walls papered in gaping clown faces. The clown hands bobbed about as if dancing under the swinging bulb. There was a cot in the middle of the room and a mobile strung with little clown bodies hung over it from a hook in the ceiling. There was a small chest of drawers, but no clothes and no toys. It was as if a baby had briefly occupied the room, but only briefly. She shut the door.

Gilda found another bedroom on the second floor. It had gabled windows and a slanted ceiling. She opened a window and looked out onto the flat tin roof of the extension. This was overhung by the sycamore which spread its branches over the roof, swirling and brushing the surface. Maybe the swishing was the noise she'd heard. She assured Archie that this bed was decent enough, sheetless but with a mattress in reasonable condition. She closed the window, took the sleeping bag out of her holdall, and laid it on the bare mattress, too tired to perform her ablutions. Without even cleaning her teeth she slid into her padded shroud and dropped into sleep.

An hour later Gilda and Archie sit bolt upright in bed shrieking and clutching each other. The window is wide open and a wailing caterwaul fills the room. Heart flailing, aware now that Archie isn't here and she is on her own, Gilda feels a blow. Something lands violently in her lap for an instant, knocking her off balance and scratching her thigh as it goes. It vanishes out of the swinging casement.

A peeping sound can still be heard in the room, perhaps a feline offering taken from a nest in the sycamore. A breathing baby chaffinch lies bloody on the bedroom floor, entrails sliding through a crack in the boards. Tight-lipped, Gilda scoops up the damp ball of feathers. She carries it gently down two flights of stairs and opens the kitchen door. Then she pries a loose brick from a border, says she's sorry, and smashes the baby skull against a concrete patio slab. Six days to go.

On the fifth night, she has run out of food and there's nothing left but a bottle of brandy she finds in the back of the cupboard where the cat food lives. Gilda hasn't had a full night's sleep all week, and the cat has never made more than a second's appearance. It makes a wild dash through the house now and then, leaving a token here or there, entering and leaving through any window or crack. Mysteriously, it appears sometimes when the windows are locked. The litter tray has not been used again.

Archie has stopped talking to Gilda. She can't seem to make him listen either. She's heard the audio book she had loaded on her phone several times, and Maureen is offhand or out when she rings the office. Now she sits in the easy chair, swigs the brandy, and when the bottle is half-empty she slides backward into blackness. Her head lolls, her mouth falls open, and her knees slide apart. She fails to hear the *ping* meant to alert her to Maureen's text.

'The owner is a creepy guy. He called me and said he got the dates wrong. Left a day early and he's coming back tonight just after midnight. Get your act together and clear off. Leave the key on the kitchen table.'

Entering silently through the well-oiled gate, passing by a child-sized mound under a bush at the edge of the garden, past the deep and putrefying pond, a bulky man's shape approaches the house. The locks turn easily, quietly.

Gilda's body tenses even before she can see. Her eyes seem stuck together and as they open, it feels as if the inner lids are lined with fine sandpaper. Her tongue is so dry she can hardly move it, and her scream issues from somewhere deep in a dry throat.

What she seems to see in the dim light is a mountain of dark fur, bearing in its front paw a bottle of brandy. The bottle is gripped by its neck, the contents slopping as it swings. A foul smell reaches her, of fermented dog's breath and bad teeth. The shape regards her, and speaks.

'Who are you and what the fuck are you doing in my house?' The voice is an ursine rasp, unlike any creature that ever lived in a house. The hulk takes a step nearer. 'And who's been at my Remy Martin?'

Gilda is too frightened to stammer. Her voice emerges strangled from her dry throat. Almost inaudibly she answers, 'I'm from PetPals.'

The face grimaces and shows the incisors in its upper jaw. The bottle is placed on the floor and the shape leans in towards her. Gilda shrinks back in the chair, drawing up her knees and choking in the reek of its breath. Fingers close around her neck, thumbs digging into her windpipe. Gilda's eyeballs swell and vision fails. The last thing she sees is a pair of huge black pupils staring into her.

From behind the chair a spotted white streak hurls itself forward over Gilda's shoulder and grasps the creature's face. A feline war cry fills the room as the claws of all four feet extend deep into the flesh of the stinking face in its fur collar. The grip on Gilda's throat releases.

Seconds later Gilda, shaking, thinks how fast you can sober up when you're in fear of your life. She finds she has slid out from under the man in the furry coat, and grasped the brandy bottle by its neck. She has just learned that half a bottle of vintage cognac can break a skull without breaking itself. Blood oozes from the claw marks at the sides of the head, and gushes from the back.

She finds her phone and calls an ambulance, her croaking voice making it hard for them to understand, 'and police,' she squeaks, rubbing at her neck.

'Thank you, puddy, for saving me,' she says to the cat, putting the phone in her pocket. 'I guess you didn't like that smell either.'

The cat crouches on the Persian rug, its eyes golden in the lamplight. It says, 'Urp,' and vomits the tail end of a shrew onto the carpet.

Hours later, sober now, Gilda is in her car talking to Archie. 'Would you believe it? Worst job I ever had,' she says, addressing a coffee mug filled with his ashes. 'I'll tell Maureen not to accept any more bookings from there, ever. A purring ball of fur dozes in a box on the back seat. The box is lined with Gilda's sleeping bag.

# MAXIMUM SECURITY

Leaving the ward, Monica's menopausal daughter speaks into an iPhone. 'It looks like she's got a broken wrist and possibly a concussion. They're keeping her in overnight,' Pause. A chattering sound in her ear. 'No, of course she's conscious. No, I'm on my way home. What? Actually, she probably fell over drunk. What can you see on the CCTV? Nothing at all? What do you mean, nothing? Never mind, I'm on my way. Bye.' She wipes her forehead with a tissue and is gone from our story.

Monica, Helen and Katty were breaking the law. At least they thought they were. Maybe. The second page of the newspaper lining the pedal bin in Monica's kitchen seemed to be telling her that current guidelines from the Department of Whatever say that only two households may meet indoors unless two or more are together in a support bubble with each other in which case they may meet with no more than one other... or was it one other household? Monica was finding it difficult to keep up. Besides, they'd agreed to bring their own sandwiches so nothing would be sticky and all she had to do was provide the drinks.

Helen read the same guidelines in her paper and was sure she'd understood it all. But virus or no virus she was tired of it, she missed her friends and it looked like rain. No patio picnic today. It was indoors or call the whole thing off and she was buggered if she was going to do that. (Not a word she'd have said out loud).

She made herself a sandwich of the best cheddar in the county (it had a politically suspect name: 'The Black Bomber'). She used a white bloomer which she sliced precisely and buttered with the brand they called The President. She added some purple-tipped lettuce from the garden as well. Wrapped it up in greaseproof, tied it with brown string and made a bow on top. She added a packet of apple crisps and assembled the whole in a sandwich box she and Harvey had bought in a National Trust gift shop. That must have been six years ago when he was still alive.

She went into the hallway and checked herself in the full length mirror. Floral blouse with the collar just peeping over the top of a 10% cashmere crewneck, pleated trousers of a barely detectable Scots plaid wool mix, and lace-up Ecco's. Nice for the autumn. She picked up a blazer (just in case) and a brolly (ditto).

Then she shivered. Meeting Katty and Monica… *indoors*? She shut her door, locked it, checked it, and noted that if Harvey were still alive, he'd never have let her go. He'd have been 'shielding'. She checked her bag for antiseptic wipes and got in the car.

Less than a mile away, Katty pushed up her long sleeves and stuck a table knife deep into a jar of Whole Earth crunchy peanut butter. It was luscious, *pinguid*. She swirled her knife around to get the oil mixed deep into the peanut butter, lifted the dripping knife and spread the peanut butter on a slice of multi-seeded wholemeal bread. She selected another slice and laid it beside its mate, indulged herself a little further with a scrape of Kerrygold and over that, a lumping spoonful of Geeta's Mango Chutney. She popped the two together.

Katty would've liked to think Geeta was a real person, running a restaurant somewhere where she could go and order a biryani featuring chunks of cinnamon bark and bits of cloves in it and on the side, a Kingfisher beer sweating with cold. Now that would be nice…. Meanwhile, sarnies at Monica's would have to do. She pushed her mane of curly grey hair out of her eyes, let one sleeve drop down to the wrist, and peered down at boots whose toes only were visible beneath a tummy somewhat expanded during months of lockdown. She'd better get going. Signing for the parcel delivery had distracted her. She'd forgotten she was observed until her phone rang. 'Mother, who was that?'

'Who was who?'

'That man, at your door.'

'Oh god Jeffery, I'd forgotten you can see on your phone who's at the door.' If only he knew. Now she was doing something riskier than opening her front door. She almost giggled.

Was it ok to meet Monica and Helen indoors? Well it was going to have to be. She set off on foot, swinging a Peruvian book bag with her sandwich and a carob bar bouncing about inside.

At home, somewhat nervously waiting for her visitors, her first *indoor visitors*, Monica checked the fridge. Yes, two bottles of Pinot Grigio were still there, nice and cold. She put a finger against the side of one bottle. Arctic. Good…. And there was a Burgundy on the table already. She shook a packet of crisps into a salad bowl and set it on a table covered by an embroidered linen cloth she'd bought in a market on Gran Canaria. She put out napkins and cutlery no, not *that* cutlery. Do people need cutlery? Well, not spoons. And let's use the nice cutlery…. She lifted a box from the sideboard and selected three knives and three forks just in case. One knife had a smudge on it. She blew on the smudge and wiped it on the hem of her skirt. That looked better.

She stood back and admired her arrangements. The table setting showed up her silverware nicely, and the light caught the shine from the knives and forks on the table right up to the antique silver ladle on the top shelf of the dresser.

She looked again at the table and frowned. It occurred to her that her friends wouldn't want to take crisps out of a big salad bowl because the virus might have crept in amongst the crisps. She got three pudding bowls out and picked up the crisps with paired hands, redistributing them into separate bowls. (They'd never know.) But she felt guilty about breathing on that table knife, the one she'd wiped on her skirt. Which knife was it? She was that nervous she picked up the wrong one and scrubbed it under a hot tap, drying it with a paper towel.

Paper towels? Oh, that's right: put some in the bathroom with the disinfectant spray. Her hands shook a little when she checked herself in the small mirror in the kitchen. The calf-length Marks & Spencer skirt and maroon pullover were a little dowdy, she admitted. These days shopping in town was too exhausting and anyway not permitted. Ordering online was … oh just impossible.

There was a loud rap at the back door and she jumped. Not to be overlooked, they had crept round through the garden.

'Hello, hello! Come in, oh! You're there, too. Good, good. D'you want to hang your jacket here, look, you know where the hook is, just here, yes.' Monica was babbling as babies babble, prior to saying anything that makes sense. Her friends knew what to do with their coats. They could remember back to March of last year when they visited back and forth all the time before *all this*.

They were hesitating in the doorway. She backed off. Katty took a step forward. She was through the door. Helen had two choices. She put a foot forward, and was over the threshold.

They were in. She sat them down in the garden room where they perched on opposite sides, clinging, as it were, to the walls. Nesting tables were beside them, coasters placed in the centre of each one. Monica produced a couple of bottles. 'Red or white?'

'Ooh, white,' this was Katty, grateful.

'Just a half a glass,' said Helen, 'I'll nurse it.' She was about to add, 'I'm driving,' but for some reason checked herself. They each took a sip and said Cheers.

Monica made a little noise like a sigh. She took a small gulp. Their bags of sandwiches leaned against the chairs where they sat. And sipped.

It must have been an hour later, maybe two, when they finally got around to poking open their sandwich bags. At some point they had migrated to Monica's large kitchen dining room. Somewhere in the slanting afternoon light, Helen had agreed to get a taxi home. Her Ecco's were unlaced and she sat at Monica's ample kitchen table in her sock feet.

Both Katty's elbows were on the table, one wide sleeve a little damp. It had trailed the surface of a glass of Pinot. This must only have been her… third glass?

Monica leaned back, her hips forward on the edge of her chair, glass in hand, slouching. They had begun their lunch well-spaced apart. But it was difficult to hear, and not all that cosy when you're sitting yards away from your friends. Gradually they had shifted their chairs and were nearly elbow to elbow.

'One thing I miss these days is going to the hairdresser and sitting under the dryer, 'Monica was in nostalgic mood. The girl would put the rollers in and lead you to the big silver beehive, funny how the hairstyles were beehive shape just like the dryers. They made a hum and you read Vogue if you'd bought it and brought it with you and if not, there was always the Woman's Own. Nowadays everything's different.'

'Everything's… digital,' mused Helen.

They began discussing surveillance. Disclosures flowed.

'So my phone went and it was Jeremy asking who had rung my doorbell. Who was that man, and what was I signing?' said Katty. 'I had to tell him it was a delivery.'

'You're saying he'd got a camera wired to your doorbell so his phone rings or something if anybody comes to your door?' Monica let out the sort of sound a mule would make if mules could laugh. 'What if you took a lover? Has he got your bedroom window wired up as well? What about the French doors at the back?'

Helen cleared her throat. 'If there was a lover he wouldn't be able to cross the garden at the back of my house. The security lights my kids have hung up there are so bright that it wakes the neighbours if a hedgehog steps on the lawn.' Monica took a slug of the Burgundy and put it down, making a purple ring on the linen cloth. 'You'd think he was checking in case I made a run for it,' said Helen.

Katty threw back her head and let out a belly laugh, glass in hand. 'It seems like our kids aren't visiting us much in the lockdown. They don't have to. I hardly see Jeremy these days…' she gazed at the ceiling, trying to think when was the last time she'd seen kids 'in real life'.

On the ceiling she saw something that looked like a light fitting with a long plastic tube sticking out of it. It had an eye at the bottom end, looking down into the room. She squinted, tipped her head back to see better, and almost unbalanced the chair. Her neck strained. The thing wasn't at the centre of the ceiling where an overhead light would be. It was at the side, so that the appurtenance resembling an eye had a full sweep of the room.

'What's that?'

'Uh, it's a camera,' said Monica, embarrassed. 'Andrew and Angela insisted on it. Well, Angela insisted and Andrew came round with a pair of steps and drilled holes at the top of the wall to put it in. I said no at first. I don't want it, I said. But they kept telling me they couldn't be coming round here to check if I'm all right and I sometimes put the phone on silent and forget to look at it because, you know – I can't be bothered – and neither can they, when it comes to it.' She took a deep drink, finishing off half a glass. She poured herself a top up, and one for Katty. It dripped a little on her skirt.

'Really?' Helen murmured.' They could be watching us right now?' She put her glass down. Her expression said, 'At any moment they could come over and find us all here together.' It didn't need to be said.

'That's it!' Monica scraped her chair away from the table and took a pouffe from its place by her wingback recliner. She dragged her dining chair over to the sideboard while the other two watched, gaping slightly. With the staggering passion of an old lady under the influence, she put the pouffe beside the chair, stepped onto its foamy top and from there, onto the chair. She stood for a moment to get her balance and then, arms flapping, she stepped up onto the sideboard. She reached up on her very tip toes and using the silver ladle from the display shelf above, Monica whacked the camera down. It clattered to the floor, wires hanging crazily from the point where the wall met the ceiling. Sparks fizzed.

There was a moment's silence. Then, 'Good for you!!!' rang out in unison from the other two. Monica shouted 'Whoopee' from the sideboard, grasped the shelf for balance, and with shaking knees, let herself down onto the chair. She was radiant in victory. She stepped off the chair and onto the pouffe.

The pouffe, all velvet and buttons and foam, tipped sideways as pouffes do, and straight down she came, wrists, forehead, and elbows— still dizzy with victory and still laughing.

It wasn't 'til the pain hit her that Monica let forth a shriek and blacked out. Katty grabbed the phone and didn't know what came next 'What *do* you do? Has it got a password? It's not doing anything.'

Helen fumbled a phone out of her bag, knocking her National Trust lunchbox out of the way, and managed to dial 999. What could she say?

You can guess the rest.

Note: The gerontechnology website ncbi.nlm.gov/pm quotes from a study by Linda Boise et al which states, 'Willingness of older adults to share data and privacy concerns after exposure to unobtrusive home monitoring [systems] raised objections after one year… despite mild cognitive impairments.'

# ACKNOWLEDGEMENTS

Thanks are due to my trusted reader and brilliant friend Kate Groom for her fearless, insightful critiques of earlier drafts of the work.

Grateful thanks also to Peppy Barlow, playwright and tutor, for her immensely helpful suggestions, encouragement and unique listening skills.

Grateful thanks to Vivian Whelpton for her insight and encouragement.

The artist Nicki Holt of Framlingham, Suffolk who kindly read and commented on the stories. Nicki offered me a wonderful image for the cover (she must be psychic.) The final result is an adaptation of her original design.

And finally, thanks to Tony Cutting for technical help without which this book would not exist, and to Subhash Chatterjee of ONE SC MEDIA LTD for further technical assistance.

# A NOTE ON THE AUTHOR

Marti Lauret was born in New York City and taken as a baby by her mother to Charleston, South Carolina where she was raised. She also spent periods of her life in Virginia, and various other parts of the United States. She moved to England in 1963 and worked as a shop assistant, law clerk, bean picker, waitress, newspaper advertising rep, and health care assistant. In 1980 she qualified as a social worker and retired in 2015. She began writing at the age of 73. Marti Lauret lives in Woodbridge, Suffolk and has one son and daughter-in-law and three talented granddaughters. The rest of her family still lives in South Carolina.

Printed in Great Britain
by Amazon